T0346861

# Tactics for TOEIC®
## Listening and Reading Test

### Practice Test 1

IIBC

**OXFORD**

# OXFORD
UNIVERSITY PRESS

Great Clarendon Street, Oxford OX2 6DP

Oxford University Press is a department of the University of Oxford.
It furthers the University's objective of excellence in research, scholarship,
and education by publishing worldwide in

Oxford  New York

Auckland  Cape Town  Dar es Salaam  Hong Kong  Karachi
Kuala Lumpur  Madrid  Melbourne  Mexico City  Nairobi
New Delhi  Shanghai  Taipei  Toronto

With offices in

Argentina  Austria  Brazil  Chile  Czech Republic  France  Greece
Guatemala  Hungary  Italy  Japan  Poland  Portugal  Singapore
South Korea  Switzerland  Thailand  Turkey  Ukraine  Vietnam

OXFORD and OXFORD ENGLISH are registered trade marks of
Oxford University Press in the UK and in certain other countries

ISBN: 978 0 19 452955 6

Printed in China

ACKNOWLEDGEMENTS

*The author and publisher would like to thank Sheridan MacInnes for writing the
answer key.*
Cover Photos: Getty Images (Flying Colours Ltd/Photodisc,
Klaus Vedfelt/DigitalVision).

*The publisher would like to thank the following for permission to reproduce
photographs:* OUP (Gene Parulis, OUP).

# Contents

**Test of English for International Communication**

**General Directions**

This test is designed to measure your English language ability. The test is divided into two sections: Listening and Reading.

You must mark all of your answers on the separate answer sheet. For each question, you should select the best answer from the answer choices given. Then, on your answer sheet, you should find the number of the question and fill in the space that corresponds to the letter of the answer that you have selected. If you decide to change an answer, completely erase your old answer and then mark your new answer.

## LISTENING TEST

In the Listening test, you will be asked to demonstrate how well you understand spoken English. The entire Listening test will last approximately 45 minutes. There are four parts, and directions are given for each part. You must mark your answers on the separate answer sheet. Do not write your answers in your test book.

## PART 1

**Directions:** For each question in this part, you will hear four statements about a picture in your test book. When you hear the statements, you must select the one statement that best describes what you see in the picture. Then find the number of the question on your answer sheet and mark your answer. The statements will not be printed in your test book and will be spoken only one time.

**Sample Answer**

Ⓐ Ⓑ ● Ⓓ

**Example**

Statement (C), "They're standing near the table," is the best description of the picture, so you should select answer (C) and mark it on your answer sheet.

**1.**

**2.**

*GO ON TO THE NEXT PAGE*

**3.**

**4.**

**5.**

**6.**

*GO ON TO THE NEXT PAGE* ➡

**7.**

**8.**

**9.**

**10.**

*GO ON TO THE NEXT PAGE* ➡

## PART 2

**Directions:** You will hear a question or statement and three responses spoken in English. They will not be printed in your test book and will be spoken only one time. Select the best response to the question or statement and mark the letter (A), (B), or (C) on your answer sheet.

**Sample Answer**

**Example**

You will hear:          Where is the meeting room?
You will also hear:    (A)    To meet the new director.
                               (B)    It's the first room on the right.
                               (C)    Yes, at two o'clock.

The best response to the question "Where is the meeting room?" is choice (B), "It's the first room on the right," so (B) is the correct answer. You should mark answer (B) on your answer sheet.

11.   Mark your answer on your answer sheet.

12.   Mark your answer on your answer sheet.

13.   Mark your answer on your answer sheet.

14.   Mark your answer on your answer sheet.

15.   Mark your answer on your answer sheet.

16.   Mark your answer on your answer sheet.

17.   Mark your answer on your answer sheet.

18.   Mark your answer on your answer sheet.

19.   Mark your answer on your answer sheet.

20.   Mark your answer on your answer sheet.

21.   Mark your answer on your answer sheet.

22.   Mark your answer on your answer sheet.

23.   Mark your answer on your answer sheet.

24.   Mark your answer on your answer sheet.

25.   Mark your answer on your answer sheet.

26.   Mark your answer on your answer sheet.

27.   Mark your answer on your answer sheet.

28.   Mark your answer on your answer sheet.

29.   Mark your answer on your answer sheet.

30.   Mark your answer on your answer sheet.

31.   Mark your answer on your answer sheet.

32.   Mark your answer on your answer sheet.

33.   Mark your answer on your answer sheet.

34.   Mark your answer on your an swer sheet.

35.   Mark your answer on your answer sheet.

36.   Mark your answer on your answer sheet.

37.   Mark your answer on your answer sheet.

38.   Mark your answer on your answer sheet.

39.   Mark your answer on your answer sheet.

40.   Mark your answer on your answer sheet.

**Directions:** You will hear some conversations between two people. You will be asked to answer three questions about what the speakers say in each conversation. Select the best response to each question and mark the letter (A), (B), (C), or (D) on your answer sheet. The conversations will not be printed in your test book and will be spoken only one time.

41. When does the conversation take place?

(A) In the morning
(B) Around midday
(C) In the late afternoon
(D) At night

42. What are the speakers waiting for?

(A) A call from a customer
(B) A job application
(C) A food delivery
(D) A contract

43. What does the woman suggest?

(A) Sending a fax
(B) Making a phone call
(C) Hiring a new manager
(D) Flying to Seoul

44. What has the woman just done?

(A) Returned from vacation
(B) Made a dinner reservation
(C) Read an interesting book
(D) Bought some house plants

45. Why does the woman thank the man?

(A) He sent her a postcard.
(B) He took care of her plants.
(C) He arranged her hotel accommodation.
(D) He painted her house.

46. What does the man give the woman?

(A) A key
(B) A hiking map
(C) Some newspapers
(D) Some water

47. When does the last interview start?

(A) At 9:00
(B) At 10:00
(C) At 11:00
(D) At 12:00

48. Who is the man planning to visit this afternoon?

(A) A client
(B) A job applicant
(C) A relative
(D) A doctor

49. Why might the woman make a telephone call?

(A) To arrange a job interview
(B) To request some paperwork
(C) To change a meeting time
(D) To purchase some supplies

50. What is the problem with the party?

(A) The weather is bad.
(B) There is a shortage of food.
(C) Space is limited.
(D) There is a scheduling conflict.

51. Why is the party being held for Maria?

(A) She received a promotion.
(B) She is retiring.
(C) She is relocating.
(D) She is getting married.

52. Where was the party originally scheduled to take place?

(A) In a restaurant
(B) In a conference room
(C) In a garden
(D) In an apartment

GO ON TO THE NEXT PAGE

53. What are the speakers discussing?

(A) A hiking trip
(B) A hiring decision
(C) A train schedule
(D) A local restaurant

54. How long ago did the man visit the place being discussed?

(A) Two days ago
(B) Two weeks ago
(C) Two months ago
(D) Two years ago

55. How will the speakers probably get to their destination?

(A) By walking
(B) By taking the train
(C) By driving
(D) By taking a bus

56. Where does this conversation take place?

(A) At a hotel
(B) At an office supplies store
(C) At a train station
(D) At a restaurant

57. What is the man looking for?

(A) A hotel room
(B) A briefcase
(C) A folder
(D) An article

58. What does the woman offer to do?

(A) Pay for breakfast
(B) Look for a lost item
(C) Organize a training session
(D) Write a magazine article

59. What is being offered at a discounted price?

(A) Financial advice
(B) Desserts
(C) Garden tools
(D) Drinks

60. Where are the speakers?

(A) At a bank
(B) At a farm
(C) In a cafeteria
(D) In a factory

61. What will the woman probably do next?

(A) Open an account
(B) Pour a cup of coffee
(C) Prepare some food
(D) Claim her order

62. Who most likely is the man?

(A) A bank representative
(B) A small-business owner
(C) A book publisher
(D) A travel agent

63. What is the purpose of the call?

(A) To request a transfer of funds
(B) To verify a travel itinerary
(C) To ask about postal rates
(D) To discuss credit card charges

64. What does the woman tell the man?

(A) She recently purchased some books.
(B) She already opened an account.
(C) She needs to send several packages.
(D) She wants to stay in London for a week.

**65.** Where do the speakers probably work?

    (A) At a university
    (B) At a power plant
    (C) At a manufacturing company
    (D) At a publishing company

**66.** What is the proposal about?

    (A) Adopting a flexible work schedule
    (B) Appointing new board members
    (C) Reducing energy costs
    (D) Recycling paper in the office

**67.** When will the proposal be presented to the board?

    (A) This morning
    (B) Next week
    (C) In two weeks
    (D) In two months

**68.** What is the conversation about?

    (A) A vacation
    (B) A television show
    (C) A coffee break
    (D) A new product

**69.** What was the problem?

    (A) An advertisement contained errors.
    (B) A device was not working.
    (C) Presenters were late for a trade show.
    (D) Some food was delivered late.

**70.** When is the trade show?

    (A) In January
    (B) In April
    (C) In June
    (D) In September

*GO ON TO THE NEXT PAGE*

## PART 4

**Directions:** You will hear some talks given by a single speaker. You will be asked to answer three questions about what the speaker says in each talk. Select the best response to each question and mark the letter (A), (B), (C), or (D) on your answer sheet. The talks will not be printed in your test book and will be spoken only one time.

71. Who is the speaker most likely calling?

   (A) Her supervisor
   (B) Her secretary
   (C) A mechanic
   (D) A salesperson

72. What problem is the speaker reporting?

   (A) A broken switch
   (B) A leak
   (C) A scheduling conflict
   (D) A travel delay

73. When does the speaker request a response?

   (A) Within a few hours
   (B) Within a day
   (C) Within two days
   (D) Within a week

74. Who most likely is the speaker?

   (A) An actor
   (B) A film director
   (C) A travel agent
   (D) A radio announcer

75. What is stated about the film?

   (A) It is a drama.
   (B) It is a comedy.
   (C) It is an adventure film.
   (D) It is a documentary.

76. When is the movie's London premiere?

   (A) On Tuesday
   (B) On Wednesday
   (C) On Thursday
   (D) On Friday

77. What is the recording mainly about?

   (A) Account information
   (B) Mailing instructions
   (C) Hours of operation
   (D) Order information

78. What will happen on January 18?

   (A) An office will be closed.
   (B) An order will be shipped.
   (C) A payment will be due.
   (D) An account will be opened.

79. How can the listener reach a customer service representative?

   (A) By calling another number
   (B) By staying on the line
   (C) By saying the word "zero"
   (D) By selecting option "nine"

80. Where is the speaker?

   (A) In a keyboard factory
   (B) At a concert hall
   (C) In a biology laboratory
   (D) At an electronics store

81. What is the speaker discussing?

   (A) An upcoming performance
   (B) Company research plans
   (C) Machine operating instructions
   (D) Factory quality inspections

82. When will the newest model probably be released?

   (A) In two months
   (B) In one year
   (C) In two years
   (D) In five years

83. What is the speaker discussing?

  (A) A product catalog
  (B) A recycling system
  (C) A document filing plan
  (D) An art display

84. When will a change in procedures begin?

  (A) On Tuesday
  (B) On Wednesday
  (C) On Thursday
  (D) On Friday

85. What is the audience asked to do?

  (A) Visit the speaker's office
  (B) Select items to order
  (C) Pick up a sheet of paper
  (D) Reorganize their offices

86. What is the purpose of the talk?

  (A) To describe the weather in Shanghai
  (B) To request that passengers board the plane
  (C) To announce a flight delay
  (D) To ask for volunteers to take a later flight

87. What will the airline give passengers?

  (A) City maps
  (B) Meal vouchers
  (C) Bus timetables
  (D) Rail passes

88. When will the bus leave the hotel?

  (A) At 6 A.M.
  (B) At 7 A.M.
  (C) At 8 A.M.
  (D) At 10 A.M.

89. What kind of company is conducting a survey?

  (A) A clothing store
  (B) A package delivery service
  (C) A suitcase manufacturer
  (D) A travel agency

90. What have customers complained about in previous surveys?

  (A) High prices
  (B) Limited choice of sizes
  (C) Crowded stores
  (D) Poor product design

91. What has the company created?

  (A) A new product
  (B) A Web site
  (C) A catalog
  (D) An instruction manual

92. Who most likely is being addressed?

  (A) Participants in a training seminar
  (B) Instructors for a writing course
  (C) Reporters at a press conference
  (D) Visitors to a museum

93. What are audience members asked to do?

  (A) Leave the room
  (B) Write a report
  (C) Pick up some papers
  (D) Introduce themselves to Mr. Chang

94. What will Mr. Chang probably do?

  (A) Describe a recent event
  (B) Distribute course materials
  (C) Introduce a speaker
  (D) Discuss sales techniques

*GO ON TO THE NEXT PAGE*

**95.** Who most likely is the speaker?

(A) A waiter
(B) A restaurant customer
(C) A chef
(D) A radio food critic

**96.** What does the speaker say about the vegetables?

(A) They are steamed.
(B) They are inexpensive.
(C) They are not available.
(D) They are locally grown.

**97.** What does the speaker ask for?

(A) A beverage order
(B) A bill
(C) A restaurant menu
(D) A recipe

**98.** Who most likely is Ms. Dai?

(A) An advertising salesperson
(B) A photographer
(C) A receptionist
(D) A writer

**99.** What does the caller ask Ms. Dai to bring with her?

(A) A portfolio
(B) A list of references
(C) A résumé
(D) A cover letter

**100.** When will the interview most likely take place?

(A) On Monday
(B) On Wednesday
(C) On Thursday
(D) On Friday

**This is the end of the Listening test. Turn to Part 5 in your test book.**

# READING TEST

In the Reading test, you will read a variety of texts and answer several different types of reading comprehension questions. The entire Reading test will last 75 minutes. There are three parts, and directions are given for each part. You are encouraged to answer as many questions as possible within the time allowed.

You must mark your answers on the separate answer sheet. Do not write your answers in your test book.

## PART 5

**Directions:** A word or phrase is missing in each of the sentences below. Four answer choices are given below each sentence. Select the best answer to complete the sentence. Then mark the letter (A), (B), (C), or (D) on your answer sheet.

101. Ms. Walters ................ to another branch, so your new financial advisor will be Mr. Merenda.

(A) transfer
(B) transferring
(C) has transferred
(D) transferable

102. The restaurant on Main Street offers a wide selection of gourmet desserts ................ several regions of the world.

(A) with
(B) by
(C) from
(D) until

103. ................ interested in viewing an apartment should contact the property manager to arrange an appointment.

(A) These
(B) Those
(C) This
(D) That

104. A growing ................ in the cosmetics industry is the use of natural and organic ingredients.

(A) product
(B) scent
(C) sale
(D) trend

105. Because of its ................ melodies and upbeat rhythms, Toby Nathan's music has broad appeal.

(A) simple
(B) patient
(C) kind
(D) blank

106. The park service asks visitors to behave ................ and show respect for wildlife.

(A) responsibly
(B) responsible
(C) responsibility
(D) responsibilities

GO ON TO THE NEXT PAGE

**107.** It is not the company's policy to grant sick leave ................. overtime pay to part-time employees.

(A) yet
(B) if
(C) but
(D) or

**108.** The ................. of the Board of Directors is scheduled for Monday.

(A) election
(B) elected
(C) elects
(D) electable

**109.** Last year, the number of new university-level textbooks ................. by American publishers dropped for the second year in a row.

(A) priced
(B) sold
(C) marked
(D) instructed

**110.** Traffic congestion is ................. than usual because of road construction, so it will take us at least an hour to get to the meeting.

(A) badly
(B) bad
(C) worst
(D) worse

**111.** Investors who lose faith in a company ................. sell off their stocks and invest elsewhere.

(A) exactly
(B) greatly
(C) approximately
(D) typically

**112.** CTC announced on Monday that a European media group is expected to ................. its online music store.

(A) buy
(B) buying
(C) bought
(D) has bought

**113.** The Tourist Board of Western Quebec is developing a marketing ................. to help them increase tourism to the region.

(A) proposal
(B) permission
(C) appliance
(D) employment

**114.** Negotiators should be aware that the Prime Minister has a very ................. manner of speaking.

(A) mutual
(B) direct
(C) adjacent
(D) existing

**115.** Jean Mallet has been selected to replace Henri Valois, ................. is retiring as president and executive officer of Marteux Pharmaceutical Corporation.

(A) that
(B) it
(C) which
(D) who

**116.** In order to suppress harmful insects and weeds, garden maintenance companies must choose the right products and apply them ................. .

(A) correction
(B) corrected
(C) correctly
(D) correcting

**117.** McGrath Publications has not published a best seller ................. Simon Porter's book *The Point* was released eight years ago.

(A) since
(B) under
(C) between
(D) during

**118.** The CEO will use her ................. in determining how the reorganization of the company will be conducted.

(A) discretionary
(B) discrete
(C) discretely
(D) discretion

119. For more than three decades, Beecham Construction has helped clients .................. their ideas into beautifully executed projects.

(A) prevail
(B) transform
(C) inspire
(D) involve

120. .................. by the audience's positive reaction to its music, the Gary Jones Band played well past midnight.

(A) Delighted
(B) Delightedly
(C) Delightful
(D) Delight

121. .................. you are buying or selling a house, be sure to use a real estate agent whose knowledge of the local market is comprehensive.

(A) Until
(B) Mainly
(C) Whether
(D) Only

122. The application process for loans from Inhouse Financing is easier than .................. , eliminating most of the typical paperwork.

(A) once
(B) never
(C) not
(D) ever

123. Income from online advertising has been growing, but is still a .................. small part of overall newspaper revenue.

(A) nearly
(B) closely
(C) precisely
(D) relatively

124. Companies that care more about customers than investors often achieve .................. growth and high rates of long-term financial gain.

(A) chief
(B) prior
(C) significant
(D) official

125. The .................. from most of our readers was positive, though many wondered why we wanted to transform a layout that was already so appealing.

(A) inquiry
(B) feedback
(C) intention
(D) hesitation

126. The houses on the street are fairly close to .................. ; however, the fences that surround each property help to ensure privacy.

(A) one another
(B) another
(C) the other
(D) other

127. The young fashion designer wanted to create dress styles .................. different from those of her contemporaries.

(A) recognize
(B) recognizing
(C) recognizable
(D) recognizably

128. The Action Shot X52 underwater camera is recommended .................. depths of up to two hundred feet.

(A) as
(B) but
(C) for
(D) out

129. Monthly reports from all divisions of the company must be delivered to the human resources office .................. by 5 P.M. today.

(A) recently
(B) promptly
(C) formerly
(D) briefly

130. Many environmental analysts recommend that nations reduce their .................. on non-renewable energy sources.

(A) dependently
(B) dependence
(C) dependent
(D) depend

*GO ON TO THE NEXT PAGE*

**131.** ................ the firm's notable achievements this past year was the opening of a new research and development center in Seoul.

(A) Into
(B) Among
(C) Despite
(D) Around

**132.** The revival of the ferry service to Seawise Island was initially viewed as a ................ notion by many, but it turned out to be profitable.

(A) mobile
(B) talkative
(C) dedicated
(D) foolish

**133.** According to a survey ................ by the Fielding Institute, advertising on the Internet accounted for 10% of total advertising.

(A) conducted
(B) conductor
(C) conducting
(D) conducts

**134.** Public speaking experts agree that it is better to express simple ideas ................ than to use complex structures with no persuasive point.

(A) comprehend
(B) comprehensible
(C) comprehensibly
(D) comprehensibility

**135.** Work in excess of 8 hours per day, ................ authorized by the client, will be invoiced at 1.3 times the regular hourly rate.

(A) when
(B) as if
(C) so that
(D) than

**136.** A particularly ................ drawback of this book is the almost complete lack of useful illustrations or tables.

(A) frustrating
(B) frustratingly
(C) frustrated
(D) frustration

**137.** From the first measurement to the last stitch, the Sagamore brothers have been ................ custom-made shirts for fifty years in their New Haven workshop.

(A) assigning
(B) calculating
(C) creating
(D) describing

**138.** Researcher Clement Chappelle was awarded £11,000 by the Ogden County Council to analyze the ................ of removing dams along the River Bourne.

(A) uncertainty
(B) feasibility
(C) quantity
(D) flexibility

**139.** In spite of the rainy weather, last evening's holiday reception was ................ attended by staff researchers and administrators.

(A) well
(B) quite
(C) many
(D) some

**140.** The Web-based marketplace is drawing thousands of customers away from leading companies, despite an ................ inflated market.

(A) even
(B) else
(C) urgently
(D) already

## PART 6

**Directions:** Read the texts that follow. A word or phrase is missing in some of the sentences. Four answer choices are given below each of the sentences. Select the best answer to complete the text. Then mark the letter (A), (B), (C), or (D) on your answer sheet.

**Questions 141–143** refer to the following memo.

To: Susan Olivieri
From: Ray Chen, Accounts Manager
Subject: Speedy Cars
Date: July 11

Enclosed please find your quarterly invoice for taxi services from April through June. Please be reminded that our rates for all trips .................. . The change in prices, which took effect on May 1, is reflected on the

**141.** (A)  are to increase
(B)  would have increased
(C)  will increase
(D)  have increased

enclosed invoice.

All checks must be made payable to Speedy Cars, Inc. Payment must be received by 5 P.M. on the indicated due date. Please mail your payment at least seven business days before the due date to ensure that it arrives on time. For all billing inquiries please call 1-800-555-5807. There is no .................. for calling this number.

**142.** (A)  complaint
(B)  record
(C)  charge
(D)  value

Thank you for trusting Speedy Cars with your business. We strive to provide quick, .................. service that takes

**143.** (A)  courtesy
(B)  courteous
(C)  courteously
(D)  courteousness

you wherever you need to go.

*GO ON TO THE NEXT PAGE*

Questions 144–146 refer to the following article.

DOCTOR NAMED TO "NOTABLE YOUNG PROFESSIONALS" LIST

Veronica Lew, M.D., of First Community Medical Center, was recently featured in a list of "Fifty Notable Young Professionals" in City News Magazine. She and the 49 others listed ................. from a list of

**144.** (A) will choose
(B) are choosing
(C) were chosen
(D) been chosen

500 candidates.

The 500 candidates had been nominated for ................. contributions to the fields of business, science and

**145.** (A) themselves
(B) their
(C) theirs
(D) them

medicine, scholarship, sports, and the arts.

Dr. Lew, a Professor of Internal Medicine, is the third physician from First Community Medical Center to be given this ................. . She is a frequent speaker at medical conferences around the world.

**146.** (A) honor
(B) amount
(C) salary
(D) pride

Her textbook, *Practicing Internal Medicine*, has just been published by Medical Publications, Inc.

**Questions 147–149** refer to the following memo.

To: Residents of Prairie Green Apartments
From: Joan Sakamoto, property manager
Date: April 8
Subject: Painting of buildings

On April 16 our building services contractors will begin repainting Prairie Green's apartment buildings. Most of their work will take place Monday through Friday between the hours of 10:00 A.M. and 4:00 P.M. Please remove all objects from your windows and balconies ............... April 16 and avoid touching the buildings'

**147.** (A) after
      (B) before
      (C) until
      (D) since

outside walls while the painting is being done.

You should ............... be cautious when leaving and entering your apartment during this time as the painters'

**148.** (A) also
      (B) once
      (C) nearly
      (D) soon

ladders might block access to doorways and steps.

We apologize for this temporary inconvenience, but we trust that you will be ............... with the results!

**149.** (A) pleased
      (B) pleasing
      (C) pleasant
      (D) pleasantly

*GO ON TO THE NEXT PAGE*

Ms. Una Vali
Director of Community Relations
Technology Systems, Inc.
Littleton, NY 11708

Dear Ms. Vali:

The New York State Department of Commerce is pleased to inform you that your organization's grant application has been accepted. Technology Systems, Inc., has been awarded $2 million to establish three technology instruction centers to provide computer facilities and classes to communities in the state. The centers will .................. more than 20,000 residents.

**150.** (A) conduct
(B) determine
(C) house
(D) serve

As agreed, each center will have its own full-time .................. , receiving a salary still to be determined.

**151.** (A) direct
(B) directed
(C) director
(D) direction

Congratulations on your .................. application.

**152.** (A) successful
(B) pending
(C) conditional
(D) revised

Sincerely,

Robert Morales

**Directions:** In this part you will read a selection of texts, such as magazine and newspaper articles, letters, and advertisements. Each text is followed by several questions. Select the best answer for each question and mark the letter (A), (B), (C), or (D) on your answer sheet.

**Questions 153–154** refer to the following advertisement.

# CREATE YOUR OWN SPACE

Do you dream of having a space away from the demands of everyday life—a place where you can create, think, and relax?

Marvel Space Planners, a group of architects, designers, and makers of built-in furniture, can turn an unused room or an awkward space into a practical room of your own. Our free, full-color brochure presents a sampling of options for individually designed spaces.

If you would like to create a customized space, why not call us today at 800-555-7552 to request a copy of the brochure or to schedule a free initial consultation with our design team.

**MARVEL**
Space Planners

**153.** What is being advertised?

(A) Rooms for rent
(B) A design service
(C) A job placement service
(D) Vacation packages

**154.** What is offered for free?

(A) Exercise equipment
(B) Some paint samples
(C) A consultation
(D) An architectural plan

*GO ON TO THE NEXT PAGE*

Theater Digest
125 Lake Ave.
Chicago, IL 60616

Dear Subscriber,

Your subscription to *Theater Digest* will end in two months. Please don't let that happen. Take time to renew your subscription today. By doing so, you will continue to receive every month the very latest in theater reviews, information on actors and directors, and up-to-date reports on new dramas and musicals for the next year.

I've attached an invoice for your renewal order. You will receive 12 issues for the special low price of $35. Please send your payment in the reply envelope provided. Make any corrections to your name or address right on the back of the invoice. Then, visit our Web site at www.theaterdigest.com to read about contests for readers. You could win tickets to a great show!

Sincerely,

*Matthew Chambers*

Matthew Chambers
Customer Service Representative

---

**155.** What is the purpose of this letter?

(A) To advertise a new publication
(B) To encourage subscription renewal
(C) To correct a billing error
(D) To request a donation

**156.** How often is *Theater Digest* published?

(A) Once a month
(B) Every two months
(C) Twice a year
(D) Once a year

**157.** What is mentioned about the Web site?

(A) It provides access to other theater-related Web sites.
(B) It offers additional information on stories printed in *Theater Digest*.
(C) It contains information about competitions for readers.
(D) It can be used for online payments.

## TRAVEL TO NACU CONFERENCE

### Airline Arrangements

Sky High Air and Mountain High Airlines will serve as the official carriers for attendees of the Forty-Fourth Annual NACU Conference. Both carriers have agreed to offer low fares for conference attendees. To obtain information on discount airfares, call Sky High Air at (800) 555-0987 and refer to Convention Number CV786309 or call the Mountain High Airlines Reservation Desk at (800) 555-7382 and refer to Convention Number HJ987.

### Ground Transportation

The trip from Rushmore Airport to downtown hotels is about 15 miles and takes 45 minutes by shuttle bus or car.

**By Shuttle Bus:** Airporter (708) 555-9541 offers a shuttle bus service from the airport to the Fairmont Hotel and the Regency Hotel. Departure time is every 20 minutes from 9:00 A.M. to 8:00 P.M. and every 30 minutes from 8:00 P.M. to 11:00 P.M. The Airporter main desk is located on the lower level, near Exit B. No reservations are required, but tickets must be purchased at the Airporter main desk, at the conference registration desk in the convention center, or at the travel agency located in the Regency Hotel. Tickets are not available directly from the shuttle bus drivers.

| Shuttle Bus One-Way Fares | | Shuttle Bus Round-Trip Fares | | By Taxi: |
|---|---|---|---|---|
| Adult | $9.00 | Adult | $14.00 | Taxis are readily available outside Exit C in the main terminal. Appropriate fare to downtown hotels is $18.00–$25.00. |
| Child | $4.00 | Child | $6.00 | |
| Family | $17.00 | Family | $26.00 | |

### Parking

For attendees driving to the conference, parking is available at both hotels. The Fairmont Hotel provides parking for $15.00 per day, with in/out privileges. The Regency Hotel offers parking for $10.00 per day Monday to Friday, $8.00 on Saturday, and $6.00 on Sunday.

**158.** On whose Web site would this information most likely be found?

(A) Sky High Air
(B) NACU
(C) Regency Hotel
(D) Airporter

**159.** The word "serve" in paragraph 1, line 1 is closest in meaning to

(A) wait on
(B) operate
(C) obey
(D) give out

**160.** How long does it take to drive to downtown hotels from the airport?

(A) 15 minutes
(B) 20 minutes
(C) 30 minutes
(D) 45 minutes

**161.** How much does it cost to park at the Regency Hotel on Thursdays?

(A) $6.00
(B) $8.00
(C) $10.00
(D) $15.00

*GO ON TO THE NEXT PAGE*

# The Ridgeway Herald News

**Black and White Display Advertisements**

| Size | 1 Month | 2 Months | 3 or More Months |
|------|---------|----------|------------------|
| Full page | $450.00 | $400.00 | $350.00 |
| 1/2 page | $250.00 | $210.00 | $180.00 |
| 1/4 page | $130.00 | $110.00 | $ 95.00 |

- Quoted prices are per month.
- One photo is included in the price of the advertisement.
- Advertisements must be received by the first of the month preceeding publication.
- Payment in full should be submitted with advertisement; payment by credit card or personal check is acceptable.

For longer-term advertising contracts, please contact Henry Shin at The Ridgeway Herald News, 87 King St., Ridgeway.

**162.** Who is this information intended for?

(A) Editors
(B) Advertisers
(C) Photographers
(D) Lawyers

**163.** What policy is stated in the information?

(A) Payment may be made after publication.
(B) Color advertisements are more expensive.
(C) A late fee may be applied.
(D) A picture may be submitted.

---

**Toppo Travel, Inc.**

Mr. Boyce Adams
424 Lenox St.
Orange, MA  01388

Dear Mr. Adams,

At the end of this year, Toppo Travel will celebrate its twentieth year as a successful operator in the leisure industry. With modern hotels, exciting itineraries, and beautiful locations, our all-inclusive, organized tours have remained the most popular in the industry for the past ten years. We have decided to include our most loyal customers in the celebration of our success.

Our records indicate that since you became a customer five years ago, you have booked six trips with us. We would therefore like to invite you to an evening of exotic fare and tropical sounds, which will be held on December 1 in the Grand Ballroom of the Panorama Hotel.

The buffet will consist of delicacies from the 16 countries that are featured in our catalog for the new season. Bands from Cuba, Mali, and Slovenia will lend an exuberant atmosphere to the event.

Enclosed please find two complimentary tickets for entry to this exclusive event.

Sincerely,

*Jim Bull*

Jim Bull
Director Customer Relations
Toppo Travel, Inc.

---

**164.** To what event has Mr. Adams been invited?

(A) A hotel's grand opening
(B) A retirement dinner
(C) An anniversary celebration
(D) An awards ceremony

**165.** For how many years has Mr. Adams been traveling with Toppo?

(A) Five years
(B) Six years
(C) Ten years
(D) Twenty years

**166.** What will the event feature?

(A) A slide show
(B) Ballroom dancing
(C) Exotic food
(D) A noted speaker

*GO ON TO THE NEXT PAGE*

**Questions 167–170** refer to the following notice.

## NOTICE TO ALDER PARK RESIDENTS:
### New City Recycling Program

On August 1, a new law will take effect in Alder Park that will require residents to recycle products made of paper, glass, and aluminum. Those recyclables should be placed in green plastic bins provided by the city, which will be delivered during the week of July 15. The city will pick up those recyclables during the first and third weeks of each month on garbage pick-up days.

Some examples of acceptable recyclables include:

| Type | Examples | Notes |
|---|---|---|
| Paper | Newspapers, printer and copy papers, magazines, envelopes, cardboard | Staples are permitted. No paper clips or plastic sheets. |
| Glass | Bottles, jars | Must be clean. Labels are permitted. Non-glass caps must be removed. No broken glass. |
| Aluminium | Cans, foils | Must be clean. Crush if possible. |

Please follow the guidelines provided above. Garbage pick-up will continue on a weekly basis, according to the regular schedule.
If you have any questions, please contact the city refuse program at 555-1067, extension 27.

167. What is announced in this notice?

(A) A revised schedule for garbage collection
(B) Fees for residential garbage pickup
(C) Rules for recycling household items
(D) The opening of a recycling center

168. Who will supply green containers?

(A) City employees
(B) Bottling company staff
(C) Recycling center volunteers
(D) Alder Park residents

169. How many times per month will papers be collected?

(A) 1
(B) 2
(C) 3
(D) 4

170. What is mentioned about bottles?

(A) They should be wrapped in newspaper.
(B) They should not be broken.
(C) They will be collected weekly.
(D) They should have no labels.

# Lasell, Inc.

676 Keenan Dr.
Fort Worth, Texas 76035

Dear Customer,

As you may be aware, Lasell has routinely received commendations for our commitment to product safety. Every item that is sold under the Lasell name is subjected to rigorous product testing. When design flaws are detected, the model is revised to eliminate the problem. In addition, our products are built from the strongest plastics to ensure that you never have a problem with a Lasell product.

In the unlikely event that products are released with previously undetected flaws, great steps are taken to ensure that every flawed item is removed from the market and replaced for customers.

Late last week, our exceptional quality assurance team identified a previously undetected minor flaw in the air filters in our 6000X model. Because our records show that you have recently purchased a 6000X vacuum cleaner, we want to inform you of this flaw and of your right to return the product for a new one. Please be assured that there is absolutely no safety risk to you or any operators of the machine. However, to ensure that you are satisfied with the quality of our products, we would like to ask you to contact the Lasell store nearest to you. The store will arrange to pick up your machine at your home at a time that is convenient for you.

Our customers' satisfaction is foremost on our mind, and we want to make sure that you are not inconvenienced in any manner. A replacement vacuum cleaner will be delivered at the time of the pickup. Furthermore, customers who share in the exchange will receive a free gift in appreciation of their business.

Sincerely,

*Joe Glidden*

Joe Glidden
Director
Customer Satisfaction Department
Lassell, Inc.

---

**171.** What is the purpose of the letter?

(A) To introduce a policy change
(B) To invite customers to an in-store event
(C) To respond to a customer complaint
(D) To announce a replacement plan

**172.** What should the reader do?

(A) Report problems immediately
(B) Pick up a gift in the office
(C) Submit a copy of the receipt
(D) Call to schedule a pickup

**173.** What is Lasell's business?

(A) Producing appliances
(B) Safety assessment
(C) Packaging materials
(D) Commercial deliveries

*GO ON TO THE NEXT PAGE*

## BRAND MANAGER                                    Juneco

**COMPANY BACKGROUND:** The Juneco Company, expected earnings of approximately $40 million, seeks to increase marketing and product innovation efforts to significantly increase revenues within 1–2 years. Headquartered in upstate New York, Juneco manufactures kitchenware products and home security systems under several nationally recognized brand names. In addition to these major brands, Juneco produces similar products under private label programs for home improvement merchants.

**RESPONSIBILITIES:** The brand manager's priority is to handle the heightening of product recognition of Juneco's major accounts abroad. The brand manager position was created to build brand recognition in the marketing sector of Juneco's new International Division. The brand manager will spearhead efforts to foster growth in garden tool products.

Specific responsibilities include the following:
- generate marketing plans and lead the development of new products;
- increase public awareness of and demand for Juneco's products;
- identify and evaluate market requirements and opportunities;
- work closely with other members of the marketing department, as well as sales and sales operations departments to ensure achievement of company goals

**PROFESSIONAL EXPERIENCE AND PERSONAL QUALITIES:** The ideal candidate will have the following qualifications:
- 3–5 years' experience as brand manager in retail marketing;
- strong experience in analyzing current markets;
- outstanding verbal and written communication skills.

**EDUCATIONAL BACKGROUND:** An MA degree in Marketing is required; an MBA is a significant plus. Upon receipt of applications, confirmation letters will be sent to applicants via e-mail. Thereafter, priority applicants will be invited to meet with Juneco's CEO and Chief Marketing Officer.

---

**174.** In which Juneco division will the successful applicant probably work?

(A) International marketing
(B) Human resources
(C) Production
(D) Accounting

**175.** What is NOT a stated job responsibility?

(A) Creating marketing plans
(B) Evaluating market opportunities
(C) Increasing product recognition domestically
(D) Working with sales representatives

**176.** The word "foster" in paragraph 2 line 4 is closest in meaning to

(A) substitute
(B) measure
(C) cherish
(D) encourage

**177.** What qualification will the successful applicant possess?

(A) Experience in the home improvement industry
(B) A degree in finance
(C) Fluency in a foreign language
(D) Experience in market analysis

**178.** How will Juneco contact applicants?

(A) By phone
(B) By fax
(C) By e-mail
(D) By mail

**Questions 179–180** refer to the following advertisement.

---

**Techno** Database
Management

5197 Blackburn Pike
Sidney, B.C., Canada V8L 5G1

**Stephanie Strickland, President**
E-mail: steph@techdatamgmt.com
Tel: 468-298-9935 / Fax: 468-298-9934
www.techdatamgmt.com

Techno Database Management provides data storage facilities for information technology and computer networking professionals. For only $39.95 per month, customers may store their data in online-accessible Web space (up to 1,000 gigabytes). For $59.95 per month, subscribers may store up to 5,000 gigabytes of data in an offline archive.

TDM customer services include 24-hour technical support and free subscription to our online bimonthly newsletter, TDM News. Topics include ratings and reviews of current software and equipment, opinion articles, and a help wanted section directed toward information technology professionals.

New customers who pay in advance for three months of offline service before July 30 will receive one month of free data storage—that's a nearly $180 value for just under $120! Call or e-mail today to set up your account.

---

**179.** About how much does three months of offline storage cost for customers who subscribe by July 30?

(A) $39.95
(B) $59.95
(C) $120
(D) $180

**180.** What is NOT featured in *TDM News*?

(A) Technical support questions and answers
(B) Discussions about computer equipment
(C) Assessments of new software
(D) Job opportunities for computer technicians

*GO ON TO THE NEXT PAGE*

## BLIXEN MEMORIAL THEATER

**Annual Fundraising Event**

January 19

Dear Friend of Blixen Memorial Theater:

As a non-profit performing arts organization, we rely on membership and fundraising efforts to support our operating costs. Every year at this time we hold a drawing to help raise funds to meet a portion of our budget.

This is your chance to help Blixen Memorial Theater. Each individual who donates $20 to the theater at this time will be eligible for a special prize. On May 20, we will select one name at random to receive this year's prize – 4 tickets to each of the 10 Blixen Memorial Theater performances for the upcoming year. (The winner need not be present.) That's 40 tickets, a $3,000 value!

To participate in this year's drawing, simply complete the entry form and mail it with your payment. We will send you a confirmation number for each $20 donation upon receipt. Every $20 you donate increases your chances of winning a whole year's worth of exciting performances. And even if your name is not selected, you'll still win by helping Blixen Memorial Theater offer high-quality programs.

For further information, call the office at (507) 555-8826, ext. 908.

Sincerely,

*Anna Kessler*

Anna Kessler
Executive Director

---

Name   Anton Maldonado

I have enclosed a check for $ _____     Address   14 Sunset Drive

Please charge my credit card   **$40**     City   Stockton     State   MN     Zip   55988

Card #   1122334455667788     Phone   507-555-2292

Signature   Anton Maldonado

Please return this form with payment to:

**BLIXEN MEMORIAL THEATER**
**Attention: Raffle**
**480 Sioux St.**
**Winona, MN 55987**

---

**181.** Why did Ms. Kessler write this letter?

    (A)   To invite Anton Maldonado to an event
    (B)   To advertise a new show
    (C)   To explain a new ticketing policy
    (D)   To announce a fund-raising event

**182.** What does Ms. Kessler say about the Blixen Memorial Theater?

    (A)   It has had to reduce its budget.
    (B)   Its next season begins on May 20.
    (C)   It holds an annual drawing.
    (D)   It is offering discount tickets to people who donate money.

**183.** What prize is being offered?

    (A)   A check for $3,000
    (B)   A year's worth of theater tickets
    (C)   Front-row seats to four performances
    (D)   Meetings with performers after the shows

**184.** In the letter, the word "present" in paragraph 2, line 4 is closest in meaning to

    (A)   in attendance
    (B)   current
    (C)   on hold
    (D)   performing

**185.** What does Anton Maldonado indicate on the form?

    (A)   He will purchase tickets to two shows.
    (B)   He will contribute to the theater.
    (C)   He is paying by personal check.
    (D)   He would like a schedule for the new season.

*GO ON TO THE NEXT PAGE*

**Questions 186–190** refer to the following e-mail and invoice.

| To: | Scott Abernathy <sa@zenith.com> |
| --- | --- |
| From: | Mike O'Malley<momalley@communicate.com> |
| Subject: | Shipment |
| Date: | June 22 |

Hi Scott,

I'm glad I was able to reach you on the phone today before you shipped my order. As I mentioned, I'd like to change the delivery date to Thursday. In addition, instead of shipping the entire order to our warehouse, please send 10 of the 50 silk lamp shades and 10 of the parchment lamp shades to the showroom on Congress Avenue.

By the way, I want to thank you again for recommending me to Vincent Balasco as a potential supplier for his furniture stores. We're meeting at the Congress Avenue showroom over the weekend so that he can have a look at the lamps, which is why I'll need the shades there. I'll let you know how it goes. Please send me a revised shipping order.

Best regards,

Mike

---

## SHIPPING ORDER

**CARRIER:** Metro Trucking
**BILL DATE:** June 23  **SHIP DATE:** June 26

| TO | | FROM | |
| --- | --- | --- | --- |
| Name | Mike O'Malley | Shipper | Zenith Lamp Part Warehouse |
| Company | Bright Lights Warehouse | Street | 3387 South Ferry Road |
| Street | 10649 Industry Road | City, State | Marshfield, Massachusetts |
| City, State | Boston, Massachusetts | Contact | Scott Abernathy |

| SEND INVOICE TO | | SHIPPER'S INSTRUCTIONS |
| --- | --- | --- |
| Name | Mike O'Malley | **SPLIT ORDER** |
| Company | Bright Lights Showroom | Deliver 10 silk shades, 10 parchment shades |
| Street | 1305 Congress Avenue | (separately packaged) to billing address. |
| City, State | Boston, Massachusetts | Deliver rest of order to Industry Road address. |

| NO. SHIPPING UNITS | DESCRIPTION OF ARTICLES | SIZE | UNIT PRICE $ | TOTAL CHARGE $ |
| --- | --- | --- | --- | --- |
| 50 | Pleated silk shade, soft white | 15 inches | 12 | 600 |
| 50 | Parchment shade, beige | 18 inches | 10 | 500 |
| 120 | Brass sockets, 3-way turn knob | Medium T-14 | 3 | 360 |
| | | | TOTAL | $1,460 |

*Hi Mike,*
*Here's the revised shipping order. Good luck showing the lamps on Saturday. I think*
*you'll like Vincent Balasco.*
*Scott*

**186.** Why did Mike O'Malley contact Scott Abernathy?

(A) To cancel a shipment
(B) To change a shipping order
(C) To invite him to the factory
(D) To place a furniture order

**187.** On which day will Vincent Balasco visit the showroom?

(A) Thursday
(B) Friday
(C) Saturday
(D) Sunday

**188.** Why will part of the order be delivered to a different location?

(A) Mike O'Malley wants to show his merchandise to a potential buyer.
(B) The Industry Road Warehouse will be closed.
(C) The Congress Avenue showroom is closer to the Zenith warehouse.
(D) Mike O'Malley is opening a second showroom.

**189.** Who is Vincent Balasco?

(A) A warehouse clerk
(B) A furniture store owner
(C) A lamp shade manufacturer
(D) A truck driver

**190.** How much is the total cost of the merchandise?

(A) $360
(B) $500
(C) $600
(D) $1,460

*GO ON TO THE NEXT PAGE*

## Lemont Valley Hospital Volunteer Program
NO EXPERIENCE NECESSARY!

**Requirements:**
- Proof of age (must be at least 18 years old)
- Satisfactory recommendation from current or former employer
- Properly completed application forms
- Ability to fulfill the commitment of one shift per week for the duration of the program session – summer, fall, or spring
- Adequate transportation to and from the hospital
- Neatness in appearance (volunteers must purchase a uniform)
- Mandatory completion of the volunteer orientation/training

**Attendance:**
A required commitment of at least one shift per work week is expected from each volunteer for the duration of the specific program session. Fall and spring four-hour shifts are available after 2:00 P.M. and on weekends. During the summer session the shifts are six hours in length Monday through Friday and four hours on Saturdays and Sundays. Individual schedules/assignments will be determined by the volunteer coordinator during the orientation on May 22.

May 15 is the deadline for summer volunteer applications.
Contact Russ Lehman at rlehman@lvh.org for more information on how to apply.

| To: | Russ Lehman <rlehman@lvh.org> |
|---|---|
| From: | Josh Tobin <jtobin@hello.com> |
| Date: | May 17 |
| Re: | Volunteering |
| Attachments: | Application, Recommendation letter |

Dear Mr. Lehman:

My name is Josh Tobin. Two weeks ago I saw the announcement for the volunteer positions posted in the weekly community newsletter.

I apologize for the delay in contacting you. I understand that the completed application was due two days ago; however, I have been out of town on vacation. I will return on May 21 and will be able to attend the orientation. Please note that all necessary documents are attached.

My time this summer is limited, but I'll be available every Tuesday. Unfortunately, I'm not available on Saturdays and Sundays due to my restaurant job. I'll wait to hear from you prior to the orientation and training next week.

Thank you for your time,

Josh

191. What is NOT required for volunteer positions?

(A) Experience working in a hospital
(B) A letter from an employer
(C) Completion of training
(D) A commitment to a weekly shift

192. On what date were applications due for summer volunteer positions?

(A) May 15
(B) May 17
(C) May 21
(D) May 22

193. What does Josh request in his message?

(A) More time to obtain a recommendation letter
(B) A specific shift in the hospital restaurant
(C) Permission to miss the orientation and training
(D) Special consideration for his late application

194. How many hours will Josh likely volunteer on the day he is available?

(A) 4
(B) 6
(C) 8
(D) 10

195. In the e-mail message, the word "limited" in paragraph 3, line 1, is closest in meaning to

(A) unavailable
(B) adequate
(C) restricted
(D) shared

*GO ON TO THE NEXT PAGE*

# Dunnlow to Deliver New Trains for Gaelic Railways

By Briana MacCorrie

Gaelic Railways (GR), the national railway, announced yesterday that it has entered into a contract with train manufacturer Dunnlow for the purchase of fourteen new electric trains. The decision by GR's management came after a test run from Rexford to Donnebrook revealed that the new trains can cover the 45 kilometers separating the two towns in half the time it takes GR's current trains.

The new trains will gradually replace those currently in service, introduced by GR 25 years ago. The railway company had originally intended to complete the project in a 5-year span so as to let the last phase of the transition coincide with the end of the 30-year life expectancy of GR's current fleet.

However, company officials were so excited by the performance of the Dunnlow trains that the decision was made to pull all current trains from the tracks within 3 years. They plan to upgrade the longest routes first, beginning with the distances longer than 100 kilometers.

Negotiations between GR and Dunnlow have been going on for nearly 2 years. The lengthy duration of the talks was mostly due to reluctance on the part of the government to help fund the project. Says Shane O'Farrel, GR's spokesperson, "We had difficulty convincing the authorities that buying new, faster trains, while expensive, was a worthwhile investment. Gradually, however, the government realized that adequate transportation is indispensable for the continued development and prosperity of the region."

## Gaelic Railways

| Service | Distance | Former Duration | New Length of Trip |
|---|---|---|---|
| Rossmoor – Kilbarney | 74 km | 1 hour and 30 minutes | 44 minutes |
| Weston – Barlow | 162 km | 2 hours and 30 minutes | 1 hour and 25 minutes |
| Southford – Kirke | 80 km | 1 hour and 40 minutes | 53 minutes |
| Rexford – Donnebrook | 45 km | 1 hour and 8 minutes | 34 minutes |

**196.** How long have the current trains been in service?

(A) 30 years
(B) 25 years
(C) 14 years
(D) 3 years

**197.** Why has the schedule been moved up?

(A) Passengers wrote to government officials.
(B) Company executives were impressed by the trains.
(C) The manufacturer offered reduced rates.
(D) The population of the area has increased.

**198.** Why did it take a long time to get the new trains approved?

(A) The expense was questioned.
(B) The design was not finalized.
(C) The company appointed a new president.
(D) The region's power supply was not sufficient.

**199.** What does Mr. O'Farrel imply about the region's economic growth?

(A) It will be difficult to sustain in the future.
(B) It will benefit from an improved transportation system.
(C) It will be slow but steady.
(D) It will depend on foreign investment.

**200.** Which train route will be upgraded first?

(A) Rossmoor – Kilbarney
(B) Weston – Barlow
(C) Southford – Kirke
(D) Rexford – Donnebrook

**Stop! This is the end of the test. If you finish before time is called, you may go back to Parts 5, 6, and 7 and check your work.**

# PRACTICE TEST 1

## TAPESCRIPTS

## PART 1

1. (A) He's lighting a fire.
   (B) He's riding a bicycle.
   (C) He's working with a wheel.
   (D) He's getting into a car.

2. (A) There's construction equipment on the field.
   (B) There are buildings by the road.
   (C) There's a lot of traffic on the highway.
   (D) There are signs along the roadside.

3. (A) The man is washing the windows.
   (B) There are trees along the edge of the street.
   (C) People are lined up to get into the building.
   (D) It's crowded on the walkway.

4. (A) They're chopping wood.
   (B) They're putting on their jackets.
   (C) They're under a tree.
   (D) They're hiking in the woods.

5. (A) The boat is leaving the dock.
   (B) The people are near some water.
   (C) The people are getting into the water.
   (D) The boat is being loaded with cargo.

6. (A) She's reading the labels on some boxes.
   (B) She's sorting mail into the slots on the wall.
   (C) She's wrapping up a package.
   (D) She's standing in line at the service window.

7. (A) The flowers have been arranged in vases.
   (B) The tables have been set for dinner.
   (C) The chairs are stacked against the wall.
   (D) The restaurant has an outdoor seating area.

8. (A) The lights are being installed above the pictures.
   (B) There's a statue in the corner.
   (C) There are many visitors in the gallery.
   (D) The pictures are mounted on the wall.

9. (A) She's trying on a shirt.
   (B) She's holding an item of clothing.
   (C) She's cleaning out her closet.
   (D) She's paying for some new clothes.

10. (A) A bridge is under construction.
    (B) A train has pulled into the station.
    (C) There are many lanes of traffic.
    (D) The people are getting out of their vehicles.

## PART 2

11. Who took my umbrella?
    (A) I'll read it later.
    (B) The blue one.
    (C) I did, by mistake.

12. Have you seen the mop anywhere?
    (A) It was nice to see you, too.
    (B) I left it in the storage room.
    (C) Put them on the top shelf.

13. Parking is expensive here, isn't it?
    (A) No, it's over there.
    (B) It just arrived.
    (C) Yes, the rates just went up.

14. Do you prefer a window or an aisle seat?
    (A) A window, please.
    (B) You can sit here.
    (C) Yes, I see it, too.

15. Why is this door unlocked?
    (A) Because I've just unlocked it.
    (B) It's by the front door.
    (C) No, not usually.

16. Take your coat with you.
    (A) I've never been there.
    (B) Is it that cold outside?
    (C) Higher than that.

17. Where should we go for dinner tonight?
    (A) I feel like having Chinese food.
    (B) Yes, we really should.
    (C) I don't have any problem with it.

18. I thought you were in New Zealand on business this week.
    (A) This is the stronger proposal.
    (B) My trip was canceled.
    (C) We appreciate your business.

19. When are you starting your new job?
    (A) For the last two years.
    (B) No, at the end.
    (C) At the beginning of May.

20. What is the new computer programmer's name?
    (A) I use a laptop.
    (B) We haven't been introduced.
    (C) I'll need a copy of the program.

21. Do you have a pencil I can borrow?

    (A)  I'm sorry, all I have is a pen.
    (B)  Yes, I took out a bank loan.
    (C)  I'll be working tomorrow.

22. Where can I find the sweaters?

    (A)  No, I don't think it is.
    (B)  On the second floor.
    (C)  Thanks, where did you find it?

23. Why don't we go to the beach this weekend?

    (A)  Sorry, I didn't know.
    (B)  That's a great idea.
    (C)  Because I was there.

24. Do we get off at the next station or the one after that?

    (A)  Yes, I think so.
    (B)  The week after next.
    (C)  Let me look at the map.

25. Don't you have to catch a ten o'clock flight?

    (A)  No, I dropped them on the floor.
    (B)  You can pick it up at the airport.
    (C)  It's been delayed until this afternoon.

26. How long should we keep notices on the bulletin board?

    (A)  About five centimeters long.
    (B)  He said it would.
    (C)  For about two weeks.

27. Why didn't you come to the party?

    (A)  I simply forgot about it.
    (B)  That's right, it didn't.
    (C)  The invitation was nice.

28. You sent that memo out last week, didn't you?

    (A)  It's an attractive scent.
    (B)  No, you told me to wait, remember?
    (C)  She was out for a few days.

29. Why didn't we get the Fujimaki contract?

    (A)  Yes, I just heard the news.
    (B)  We wanted too much money.
    (C)  No, she hasn't been contacted.

30. Can you make sure there's a slide projector in the boardroom?

    (A)  He's on the Board of Directors.
    (B)  No, not that I'm aware of.
    (C)  I've already set it up.

31. Do you know who that man was?

    (A)  I saw him, too.
    (B)  That was very meaningful.
    (C)  The new assistant manager.

32. I can drive you to the airport tomorrow if you need transportation.

    (A)  Thank you, but it's been arranged.
    (B)  Yes, I can take you there.
    (C)  That's the station over there.

33. Do you need the afternoon to finalize the budget, or can you help me plan the presentation?

    (A)  He's been planning on it.
    (B)  The finance meeting is in the boardroom.
    (C)  I should be able to help you by 3 P.M.

34. What kind of refreshments are they planning for the reception?

    (A)  Reception is bad in this area.
    (B)  Just dessert with coffee and tea.
    (C)  That was very kind of him.

35. Aren't we going to collect money for a gift?

    (A)  Yes, we should do that.
    (B)  It's so nice of you to think of me.
    (C)  I've been there.

36. How many callers responded to our radio advertisement?

    (A)  More than we expected.
    (B)  Sorry, I'll lower the volume.
    (C)  It's a four-color brochure.

37. Did you get the pay raise you asked for?

    (A)  No, I don't have any questions.
    (B)  Yes, effective as of next week.
    (C)  Yes, four people are coming.

38. Can you handle incoming phone calls while I go to lunch?

    (A)  Yes, he came in early this morning.
    (B)  No, it broke off when I dropped the cup.
    (C)  Yes, I'll be free in an hour.

**39.** Hasn't she read the market share report yet?

    (A) But she has brown hair.
    (B) She's been too busy.
    (C) I bought it in a shop.

**40.** I hear you'll be retiring soon.

    (A) Yes, in about a month.
    (B) I always get sleepy after lunch.
    (C) It's almost twelve o'clock.

## PART 3

**Questions 41 through 43 refer to the following conversation.**

**M:** I was wondering if we received the contract from Ms. Park? She said last night that she'd fax it here today.
**W:** It hasn't arrived yet. Perhaps we should call her if we don't get it by lunchtime?
**M:** Well, it's only ten o'clock in the morning, and she's very reliable. The Seoul office is running so much better since she became the manager.

**41.** When does the conversation take place?
**42.** What are speakers waiting for?
**43.** What does the woman suggest?

**Questions 44 through 46 refer to the following conversation.**

**M:** Mrs. Anderson, welcome back! How was the vacation?
**W:** It was great. I stayed at this tiny hotel by the lake, hiked during the day, and visited local restaurants in the evenings. It was wonderful. Thanks for watering my plants when I was away.
**M:** That's not a problem at all. You were such a great help when we went on vacation the last time. Oh, here are all your newspapers, by the way. We picked them up for you while you were away.

**44.** What has the woman just done?
**45.** Why does the woman thank the man?
**46.** What does the man give the woman?

**Questions 47 through 49 refer to the following conversation.**

**W:** I have a question before we call the first applicant in. Will we be done here by noon? I told a client I would meet him to discuss some business over lunch.

**M:** The last interview starts at 11 o'clock, so we should be done in plenty of time. I have a doctor's appointment this afternoon, anyway.
**W:** OK, but if it looks like that 11 o'clock interview is going to go much more than an hour, I'll need to step out to give my client a call. I might just have to ask him to reschedule.

**47.** When does the last interview start?
**48.** Who is the man planning to visit this afternoon?
**49.** Why might the woman make a telephone call?

**Questions 50 through 52 refer to the following conversation.**

**M:** If the rain doesn't stop within the next two hours, we should consider postponing Maria's retirement party.
**W:** I think it's too late to postpone it. The caterer and florist are set to arrive in an hour, so we'd better come up with an alternative to holding it in the garden.
**M:** Why don't we have them set up in the conference room instead? It's a shame to move it indoors, but what other choices do we have?
**W:** OK. I'll go to my office and call everyone to let them know that we're moving the party from the garden to the conference room.

**50.** What is the problem with the party?
**51.** Why is the party being held for Maria?
**52.** Where was the party originally scheduled to take place?

**Questions 53 through 55 refer to the following conversation.**

**W:** Dr. Chen and I are going to eat at that vegetarian restaurant by the station. Would you like to come along?
**M:** You mean the one on Logan Street? I went there about two months ago, and the service was pretty slow.
**W:** Well, I heard they hired a new manager a couple of weeks ago, so maybe it's better now. Plus, it's close enough to walk to, so we won't have to drive.

**53.** What are the speakers discussing?
**54.** How long ago did the man visit the place being discussed?
**55.** How will the speakers probably get to their destination?

**Questions 56 through 58 refer to the following conversation.**

**M:** I just checked my hotel room, and I can't find the blue folder I took to the effective training strategies session yesterday. It's not in my briefcase either.

**W:** Maybe you left it in the effective training strategies session? I think I'm attending a seminar in the same auditorium today. Should I have a look for you?

**M:** That would be nice of you, thanks. It has all the notes I took for the article I'm writing for *Pacific Business Review*.

**W:** I'll meet you back here in the hotel lobby at ten, and I'll let you know if I find it.

56. Where does this conversation take place?
57. What is the man looking for?
58. What does the woman offer to do?

**Questions 59 through 61 refer to the following conversation.**

**W:** Hi, I'd like the vegetable soup, the large salad with chicken, and a medium coffee. Oh, and a slice of chocolate cake.

**M:** That will be seven dollars and twenty-five cents. But just to let you know, we have a discount on desserts today. You can buy two pieces of pie or cake and get one free.

**W:** In that case I'll take one piece of peach pie, and two pieces of chocolate cake wrapped to go.

**M:** OK, your total is eight dollars and fifty cents. Please move to the end of the counter to pick up your order.

59. What is being offered at a discounted price?
60. Where are the speakers?
61. What will the woman probably do next?

**Questions 62 through 64 refer to the following conversation.**

**M:** This is Leo Schultz with Core Bank Credit. I'm calling to verify some unusual activity on your business credit card account.

**W:** What kind of activity? Do we need to be worried?

**M:** Well, Ms. Yamada, I wanted to confirm three large transactions made in euros, posted in Dublin. Are you aware of these international purchases?

**W:** Oh, yes. We ordered books from three different booksellers there last week.

62. Who most likely is the man?
63. What is the purpose of the call?
64. What does the woman tell the man?

**Questions 65 through 67 refer to the following conversation.**

**W1:** Ms. Wong, I had a chance over the weekend to read your proposal for cutting down on our heating costs. It looks very promising. In fact, I'd like to implement some of the changes by April or even sooner.

**W2:** Thank you, Ms. Sanchez. Do you think we should present some of my ideas at the board meeting next week?

**W1:** Definitely. I think the chairperson will be especially interested in your thoughts on using energy more efficiently.

**W2:** That's wonderful. I just want to see the university be able to spend more on educating our students and less on operating costs.

65. Where do the speakers probably work?
66. What is the proposal about?
67. When will the proposal be presented to the board?

**Questions 68 through 70 refer to the following conversation.**

**W:** How's development of the new coffeemaker going? I thought it would be ready in January.

**M:** Well, we were having difficulty with the automatic timer, but we took care of it in April.

**W:** Great! Then it should be ready for the September trade show in Paris?

**M:** Yes. Marie's already started the advertising campaign. We're running an advertisement in *Good Food Magazine* in June.

68. What is the conversation about?
69. What was the problem?
70. When is the trade show?

## PART 4

**Questions 71 through 73 refer to the following telephone message.**

Hi, Paul, this is Christine Roberts. I'm concerned that the oil pan in my car is leaking, so I wanted to see if you could take a look at it this afternoon. For the last couple of weeks, I've been noticing that my oil tends to run low, and I'm finding a bit of oil underneath the car in my garage. I hope you'll be able to get back to me soon, as I'll have to leave in two hours. If you think you could fit me into your schedule today, I could drop the car off on my way to work and you can just give me a call to let me know how much it will cost for you to fix it. My number is 555-1058. Thanks a lot. Bye.

71. Who is the speaker most likely calling?
72. What problem is the speaker reporting?
73. When does the speaker request a response?

**Questions 74 through 76 refer to the following talk.**

Good morning. This is Harold Chang for *Movie Tuesday*. In this session, I'll be interviewing Maura O'Connor, star of the new comedy film, *Forever and a Day Later*. It opens here in London on Thursday. Ms. O'Connor is known primarily as a dramatic actress. Is her career headed in a new direction? We'll get her views on doing comedy, what it's like to work with her costar Derek Jones, and her adventures while filming and traveling in Australia. So stay tuned to this station for Maura O'Connor, speaking about her role in *Forever and a Day Later*, which premieres in London on Thursday. And now, it's time for the weather and traffic report.

74. Who most likely is the speaker?
75. What is stated about the film?
76. When is the movie's London premiere?

**Questions 77 through 79 refer to the following recorded message.**

You have reached Tristar's automated account information line. Our records indicate that you have a current balance of forty-two euros. Your next payment is due on January 18th. If you would like to make a payment now, please press one. For details of the charges on your bill, please press two. To speak to a customer service representative, please press nine. To repeat these options, please stay on the line.

77. What is the recording mainly about?
78. What will happen on January 18th?
79. How can the listener reach a customer service representative?

**Questions 80 through 82 refer to the following talk.**

Now we're entering the laboratory portion of the Alyeska Electronic Piano factory. Our lab places a great deal of emphasis on both sound quality and keyboard mechanics, and we're always researching ways to approximate what a real piano does with our electronic keyboards. We've been developing our latest model for the last five years, and we expect to release it in two more years. You can imagine how labor-intensive all this research is.

80. Where is the speaker?
81. What is the speaker discussing?
82. When will the newest model probably be released?

**Questions 83 through 85 refer to the following announcement.**

Because our company is concerned about the environment, there are some changes as to how office waste will be handled. Starting next Friday, receptacles will be placed throughout the office for recycling. Please note that all red containers are for anything that is plastic, while all green containers are meant for glass items. These containers will be emptied each Wednesday and their contents sent to a recycling facility. As you leave, please take one of the papers on the table at the back of the room. It summarizes all of the information I've just given you. Remember, the program doesn't begin until Friday. Thank you for your cooperation with this effort.

83. What is the speaker discussing?
84. When will a change in procedures begin?
85. What is the audience asked to do?

**Questions 86 through 88 refer to the following announcement.**

Attention, passengers awaiting Crane airways flight 7 from Shanghai to Osaka. We regret to inform you that we must delay take-off again. We had hoped that by now the weather conditions in and around Osaka would have improved, but we're told they have not. At this time we'd like to provide hotel accommodations for all ticketed passengers. Outside terminal 6, a bus is waiting to take you to the Pavilion Hotel, where you will spend the night. Crane Airways agents will distribute meal vouchers as you board the bus. The vouchers are good for one free dinner and one free breakfast. At 8 A.M. the bus will leave the hotel to bring you back to the terminal. We have rescheduled the flight for 10 o'clock tomorrow morning. So, please be waiting out in front of the hotel tomorrow morning at 8 A.M.

86. What is the purpose of the talk?
87. What will the airline give passengers?
88. When will the bus leave the hotel?

**Questions 89 through 91 refer to the following excerpt from a talk.**

Next week, we'll begin conducting a survey to find out how much people are willing to pay for luggage. Previous surveys tell us that customers are frustrated when they can't quickly find things in their suitcases. In other words, people just don't like the way suitcases are designed. We've come up with a suitcase model that addresses that problem, but we need to find out if people are willing to pay a price high enough to make selling it profitable.

89. What kind of company is conducting a survey?
90. What have customers complained about in previous surveys?
91. What has the company created?

## Questions 92 through 94 refer to the following excerpt from a speech.

Now that our morning meet-and-greet is coming to an end, please go to the table at the back of the room to pick up your training packet, which includes course materials, articles, and biographies of our instructors. Then find a seat and take a minute to review the write-up of Mr. Yi Chang, our first speaker, to familiarize yourself with his 1-2-3 Sales! techniques before he comes out to give his seminar.

92. Who most likely is being addressed?
93. What are audience members asked to do?
94. What will Mr. Chang probably do?

## Questions 95 through 97 refer to the following talk.

Good evening, and welcome to Michael's. We're so happy to have you dining with us tonight. To start off your evening, I can recommend a fresh garden salad with your choice of dressing. Oh, and all of our garden vegetables are purchased fresh from local farmers. For our main course specials this evening, we can offer you either a choice of grilled seafood or vegetarian dishes. I'll give you a little more time to look over the menu and make your choices but, before I go, what can I get you to drink this evening?

95. Who most likely is the speaker?
96. What does the speaker say about the vegetables?
97. What does the speaker ask for?

## Questions 98 through 100 refer to the following message.

Hello, Ms. Dai. This is Marie Nakata calling on behalf of Kochimo Studios. I received your cover letter, résumé, and reference list on Monday. Your credentials seem very impressive. I contacted Ms. Ando, the editor of *Singapore Today Magazine*, and she said that the freelance work you did for the magazine was phenomenal. I would like to schedule an interview with you for Friday morning at 9 o'clock. Please bring with you a portfolio of your work so that I can have a more extensive look at the types of photos you have taken. I will be out of the office all day Thursday, so please try to contact me before then to confirm that you could come in on Friday. I look forward to meeting with you.

98. Who most likely is Ms. Dai?
99. What does the caller ask Ms. Dai to bring with her?
100. When will the interview most likely take place?

# PRACTICE TEST 1

## ANSWER KEY

**The first answer given is the correct option.**

## PART 1

1. **(C) The man is doing something to a wheel attached to a machine and there are many wheels piled up behind him, so he is probably a tire fitter. *He's working with a wheel* best describes the picture.**
   (A) The man is not *lighting a fire*.
   (B) The man is standing on the floor, not *riding a bicycle*.
   (D) The wheels may be from cars, but the man is not *getting into a car*.

2. **(A) In the picture there is a *field* with some heavy *equipment* on it, probably *construction equipment*.**
   (B) The equipment may be for constructing a *road*, but there is no road in the picture and there are no *buildings*.
   (C) The picture does not show *traffic on a highway*.
   (D) The picture does not show a *roadside* with *signs along it*.

3. **(B) In the picture there is a line of trees planted along the sidewalk next to a street, so the best description is *There are trees along the edge of the street*.**
   (A) The man in the picture is walking, not *washing the windows*.
   (C) There are no *people lined up to get into the building*.
   (D) *The walkway* is not *crowded*.

4. **(C) The picture shows some people *under a tree*.**
   (A) The people are not *chopping wood*.
   (B) Some of the people are wearing jackets, but they are not *putting on their jackets*.
   (D) The tree is not *in the woods* and the people are not *hiking*.

5. **(B) The picture shows two people on a structure over some water, so they are *near some water*.**
   (A) The picture does not show a *boat leaving a dock*.
   (C) The people are not *getting into the water*.
   (D) There is no *boat being loaded with cargo*.

6. **(A) The woman in the picture seems to be *reading the labels on* the *boxes*, so (A) best describes the picture.**
   (B) This may be a mail sorting office, but the woman is not *sorting the mail into the slots on the wall*.
   (C) She is looking at the packages, not *wrapping up a package*.
   (D) The picture does not show anybody *standing in line at a service window*.

7. **(D) The tables are outside. They have tablecloths on them and chairs arranged around them, so this is most likely the *outdoor seating area* of a *restaurant*.**
   (A) There are no *flowers in vases* in the picture.
   (B) The tables have no knives and forks, or plates and glasses on them, so they have not *been set for dinner*.
   (C) The chairs are around the tables, not *stacked against the wall*.

8. **(D) The picture is of a display of pictures on a wall, so *The pictures are mounted on the wall* best describes what we see.**
   (A) There are lights above the pictures, but they are not *being installed* now.
   (B) There is a tree in the corner, not *a statue*.
   (C) This may be a gallery, but there are **no** *visitors*.

9. **(B) The woman is standing next to a rack of clothes. *She is holding an item of clothing*.**
   (A) She is not *trying on a shirt*.
   (C) The picture is not of a woman *cleaning out her closet*.
   (D) She is not *paying for some clothes*, though she is probably in a shop.

10. **(C) The picture shows a road with *many lanes of traffic* going in different directions.**
    (A) There is a bridge over the road, but it is not *under construction*.
    (B) The picture does not show a *train* at a *station*.
    (D) The picture does not show *people getting out of their vehicles*.

## PART 2

11. **(C) The question asks who took the man's umbrella. *I did* means *I took it*.**
    (A) also answers the question *who*, but it refers to an action in the future and is about *reading* something, not *taking* something.
    (B) does not answer the question *who*.

12. **(B) The first woman is looking for *the mop*, which is a cleaning utensil. She is not sure if the other woman knows where it is. In (B) the second woman gives the location of the mop.**
   (A) does not give any information about the mop.
   (C) The second woman is giving instructions about where to put several things, *them*, not stating where a single thing, the mop, is.

13. **(C) The woman asks for confirmation of her statement about the high cost of parking in the area by using the negative question tag *isn't it?* In (C) the man agrees with *yes* and adds some information about the *rates*, probably the *parking rates*.**
   (A) is incorrect because it responds to a question about the location of something.
   (B) is incorrect because parking cannot *arrive*.

14. **(A) They are probably on a train or a plane. The first man asks which seat the other man *prefers*, or likes better. In (A) the second man states his preference for a *window* seat.**
   (B) The man is offering a seat, not answering the question and stating a preference.
   (C) Answers a question about whether the man can see something, not a question about *seat* preference.

15. **(A) The key question word is *why*, which asks the reason for something. (A) is the only response that gives a reason.**
   (B) gives the location of something, not the reason for something.
   (C) does not answer the question why.

16. **(B) In the statement, the man advises the woman to take her coat. In (B) the woman is checking whether a coat is really necessary.**
   (A) is a response to information about a particular place, so it is not appropriate here.
   (C) gives information about the best position for something, so it is not appropriate here.

17. **(A) The first speaker asks for a suggestion about the restaurant where they will have dinner. In (A) the second speaker indirectly suggests going to a Chinese restaurant.**
   (B) and (C) both answer the question of *whether* or not the two speakers should do something, not *where they should eat*.

18. **(B) The first woman is probably surprised to see the other woman because she thought she was away. In (B), the second woman explains why she is not away.**
   The first woman does not mention *a proposal*, so (A) is not correct.
   (C) The second woman is thanking the other person for her *business*. The first woman did not mention *doing business* together.

19. **(C) The key question word is *when*, so a date is the correct answer.**
   (A) answers a question about *how long* something has been happening.
   (B) does not correctly answer this *when* question.

20. **(B) The question asks for the name of the new computer programmer, probably a new colleague. In (B) the man implies that he does not know the person's name.**
   (A) states the type of computer the second person uses. The first person did not ask about this.
   (C) is about a *computer program*, not a *computer programmer*.

21. **(A) In this question, the man asks to borrow a pencil. (A) is an appropriate response if the woman only has a pen.**
   (B) When a person takes out a *bank loan*, they borrow *money* from a bank. The man asked to borrow a pencil, not money.
   (C) The question was not about what the other person will be doing tomorrow.

22. **(B) The key question word is *where*, so a location is the correct answer. The speakers are probably in a department store.**
   (A) does not answer the question *where*.
   (C) is a response you might make when somebody has found something you had lost.

23. **(B) With her question, the first woman suggests going to the beach. (B) is an appropriate way of agreeing enthusiastically to a suggestion.**
   (A) is an apology, not a response to a suggestion.
   (C) is a response to a question asking for the reason why something did or did not happen in the past.

24. **(C) The man asks the woman at which station or where they should get off. (C) is an appropriate response if the woman needs to check the map first.**
   (A) is not a correct response to a question including *or*.
   (B) is an answer to a question about *when* something will happen.

25. **(C) The man asks the question to check the time of the woman's flight. He may be surprised that the woman has not left for the airport. In (C) information about the time of the flight is given.**
(A) is incorrect because the question was not about catching objects, but about catching a flight.
(B) A person does not *pick up* a flight.

26. **(C) The question *how long* asks about the length of *time* that the notices should be kept on the board. In (C) *for* is used with a period of time to answer the question *how long*.**
(A) The man does not ask for a measurement.
(B) This choice does not answer the question *how long …?*

27. **(A) The first woman wants to know *why* the second woman *did not* go to the party. (A) is a possible reason for *not going* to a party.**
(B) *That's right* shows agreement with something the other person said, not the reason for an action. Also, *it didn't* does not respond to anything in the question.
(C) does not give a logical reason for *not* going to the party.

28. **(B) The first man is checking that the other man sent the memo last week. In (B), the other man responds that he did not send the memo and gives the reason why.**
(A) is incorrect because the question is not about *scent*, which means *perfume*.
(C) is incorrect because the question is not about another person, *she*, being out, or away.

29. **(B) A question with *why* asks for the reason for an action. In this case it asks for the reason why their company *did not get* the contract. (B) gives a logical reason for this.**
(A) This shows agreement. It does not give a reason.
(C) does not give a reason. Also, the pronoun *she* does not refer to anything in the question.

30. **(C) The question is a request for the woman to prepare some equipment. *It* in (C) refers to the equipment, which the woman has already set up.**
(A) is not an appropriate response to a request for someone to do something.
(B) is a response to a question asking *if* there is a slide projector in the boardroom.

31. **(C) The key question word is *who*. The man uses the phrase *Do you know* before it to make the question more indirect. (C) best answers the question *who*.**
(A) has the pronoun *him*, which could refer to *that man*, but it does not answer the question *who*.
(B) is about a thing, *that*, not a person.

32. **(A) The first man offers to drive the second man to the airport. (A) is a polite refusal of the offer.**
(B) This is a response to a *request* for transportation, such as "Could you please take me to the airport?" not the response to an *offer*.
(C) gives information about the location of the station. The first man did not ask for such information.

33. **(C) In the question, the woman asks for help with her presentation, but she also asks if the man needs to do other work in the afternoon instead. (C) is an appropriate response to the request for help.**
(A) refers to *he*, but a man is not mentioned in the question.
(B) This choice gives the location of a finance meeting. There is no mention of a meeting in the question.

34. **(B) The question is about arrangements for a *reception*, which is a formal social occasion. The man asks *what kind of refreshments*, or things to eat and drink, are planned, so (B) is the best response.**
(A) *Reception* means the ability to receive a radio or television signal, so it is incorrect.
(C) is in the past tense, so it cannot be a response to a question about something that is being planned.

35. **(A) The question with *Aren't we going to* implies that the woman expects that they will collect money for a gift for someone. In (A) the man agrees with the expectation.**
(B) is incorrect because it is a way of thanking somebody for a gift.
(C) ends with *there*, so it is about a place. The question is not about a place.

36. **(A) This is an appropriate answer to the question *How many callers…?***
(B) is not an appropriate response to a question about *how many*.
(C) gives a number, but it is about a *brochure*, not a *radio advertisement*.

37. **(B) The question asks if the man received the *pay raise* that he asked for. In (B), the man says *yes*, meaning he got the pay raise. *Effective as of* is used to say when the pay raise will begin.**
(A) is not about getting a pay raise.
(C) The question did not ask about the number of people coming to something.

38. **(C) The question is a request for help. The first man needs somebody to *handle*, or deal with phone calls when he is at lunch. In (C) the man agrees to help and says when he will be available.**
   (A) The question did not ask about *when* somebody came in.
   (B) The question was not about a broken *handle* on a cup.

39. **(B) The question asks whether *she*, another person, has read a particular report. (B) implies that *she* has not read the report and gives the reason for this.**
   (A) There is nothing in the question about somebody's hair color.
   (C) This response does not refer to *she* or to a business report.

40. **(A) The woman has heard the news of the man's retirement and wants to know more about it. In (A) the man confirms that he is retiring and says when.**
   (B) The woman was talking about the man *retiring*, or finishing his working life, not being *tired*.
   (C) The woman did not ask what the time was.

## PART 3

41. **(A) The man says that it's ten o'clock *in the morning*.**
   Thus, the correct answer cannot be (B) *around midday*, (C) *in the late afternoon*, or (D) *at night*.

42. **(D) The man asks if they have received *the contract* from Ms. Park and the woman answers that *it hasn't arrived yet*, so they are waiting for *a contract*.**
   (A) The woman suggests calling Ms. Park, but they are not *waiting for a call* from a customer.
   (B) The speakers do not talk about *a job application*.
   (C) They hope to receive the contract by lunchtime, but they do not mention *a food delivery*.

43. **(B) The woman says "perhaps we should call her." In other words, she suggests *making a phone call*.**
   (A) Ms. Park intended to fax the contract to the speakers, but the woman speaking does not suggest *sending a fax*.
   (C) The man mentions Ms. Park's new role as manager, but the woman does not suggest *hiring a new manager*.
   (D) *Seoul* is where Ms. Park works. The woman does not suggest *flying there*.

44. **(A) The man asks the woman about her *vacation* and she tells him what she did on her *vacation*, so she has probably just *returned from vacation*.**
   (B) The woman does not talk about *making a dinner reservation*.
   (C) The woman does not talk about *reading a book*.
   (D) The speakers mention the woman's plants, but the woman does not say she has recently *bought some plants*.

45. **(B) The woman thanks the man for *watering her plants*. In other words, he took care of them while she was away.**
   (A) Neither speaker mentions *postcards*.
   (C) The woman tells the man about the *hotel* she stayed in, but does not imply that *he arranged it for her*.
   (D) The man is probably a neighbor. There is no mention of him *painting the house*.

46. **(C) We often say "here is" or "here are" when we are giving something to somebody. The man is giving the woman her *newspapers*.**
   He does not give her (A) *a key*, or (B) *a hiking map*.
   (D) The woman thanks the man for watering her plants. He does not *give the woman some water*.

47. **(C) The conversation takes place before the first interview. The question is about the time of the last interview and the man says it starts *at 11:00*.**
   The last interview does not start at (A) *9:00* or (B) *10:00*.
   (D) The speakers hope that the last interview will be completed by *noon*, or *12:00*, but it *starts* at 11:00.

48. **(D) The man says he has a *doctor's appointment* in the afternoon.**
   (A) It is the woman who is planning to see *a client*, not the man.
   (B) Neither of the speakers is visiting *a job applicant*. The applicants are coming to their office.
   (C) There is no mention of *a relative*.

49. **(C) The woman says she might have to call her client to reschedule their lunchtime meeting, or in other words *change the meeting time*.**
   (A) The woman may *step out* of the interview, or leave the interview briefly, in order to call her client. She is not going to *arrange a job interview*.
   The woman is not going to telephone about (B) *some paperwork* or (D) *some supplies*.

50. **(A) The man suggests *postponing the party*, or holding it at a later time or date, *if the rain doesn't stop*, so the *bad weather* is the problem.**

(B) The woman mentions the caterer, but there is no mention of a *shortage* of food.

(C) There is not a problem with the amount of space for the party.

(D A *scheduling conflict* means two events have been scheduled to take place at the same time. This has not happened here.

51. **(B) The speakers are discussing *Maria's retirement party*. The party is being held because Maria *is retiring*. In other words, she has reached the age when she will finish working.**

Thus, she has not (A) *received a promotion*, or higher position, and she is not (C) *relocating*, or going to work in a different place. Nor is she (D) *getting married*.

52. **(C) The woman talks about finding *an alternative to holding it* (the party) *in the garden*, so the party was originally scheduled to take place *in a garden*.**

The man talks about moving the party indoors. (A), (B), and (D) are all indoor locations, so none of these can be the location where the party was *originally scheduled to take place*.

53. **(D) The woman invites the man to join her and Dr. Chen *at a vegetarian restaurant*. She says that it is close enough to walk to, so it is a *local restaurant*.**

They then go on to discuss whether it is a good restaurant. They are not talking about (A) *a hiking trip*, (B) *a hiring decision*, or (C) *a train schedule*.

54. **(C) The man says he went there two months ago. The word there refers to the restaurant they are discussing.**

He visited it *two months ago*, not (A) *two days ago*, (B) *two weeks ago*, or (D) *two years ago*.

55. **(A) The speakers will most likely *walk* to their destination, the restaurant, since the woman mentions the fact that *it's close enough to walk to* and therefore they *won't have to drive*.**

We can infer from what the woman says that they do not intend to get there by (B) taking the train, (C) driving, or (D) taking a bus.

56. **(A) At the beginning of the conversation the man says he *just checked his hotel room* for something and at the end the woman refers to *the hotel lobby* as *here*, so the speakers must be in the hotel.**

There is nothing in the conversation to indicate that they could be at (B) *an office supplies store*, (C) *a train station*, or (D) *a restaurant*.

57. **(C) The man says he *can't find his blue folder* and he *checked his hotel room* for it, so he is looking for *a folder*.**

(A) He is not *looking for* a hotel room, he has been *looking in* his hotel room for the folder.

(B) He *looked in* his *briefcase* for the folder, so we know he is not *looking for* his *briefcase*.

(D) The folder contains notes he made for an article. He is not looking for the article, which he has not yet written.

58. **(B) The woman asks *if she should have a look for the folder in the auditorium where the man last had it*. She is offering to *look for the lost item*.**

(A) They do not talk about having *breakfast*.

(C) They talk about a *training session* the man went to. The woman does not offer to *organize a training session*.

(D) *The man* is going to *write a magazine article*, not the woman.

59. **(B) The man says they have a *discount on desserts today*. This means *desserts* are *being offered at a discounted price*.**

(A) The man suggests how the woman might save money on her food, but he is not offering her *financial advice at a discounted price*.

(C) *Garden tools* are not being sold here.

(D) *Desserts* are being offered *at a discounted price*, not *drinks*.

60. **(C) The woman is placing a food order and the man is serving her with food, so they must be in *a cafeteria*.**

People do not generally order food (A) *at a bank*, (B) *at a farm*, or (D) *in a factory*.

61. **(D) At the end of the conversation, the man asks the woman to *pick up*, or *claim*, her order, so this most likely is what she will do next.**

(A) It is unlikely that she could *open an account* in a cafeteria.

(B) The man does not ask her to *pour* her own *coffee*.

(C) The man, who is the cafeteria assistant, will probably *prepare some food*, not the woman.

**62.** **(A)** The man gives the name of the organization he works for, *Core Bank Credit*. This and the fact that he is calling Ms. Yamada to check on *transactions on her credit card account* indicate that he is most likely a *bank representative*.

(B) It is evident that the man works for a bank, which is not *a small business*.

(C) *A book publisher* does not check on people's bank transactions.

(D) The man works for a bank, not a travel agency.

**63.** **(D)** The man states the purpose of his phone call, which is to *verify*, or check, some *unusual activity on her credit card account*. He then asks the woman whether she is *aware of*, or knows about, some purchases made in another country. Thus, he calls to *discuss credit card charges* with her.

(A) *To request a transfer of funds* means to ask to move money from one account to another. A bank customer might ask to do this, not a bank employee.

(B) The man calls the woman to verify credit card charges, not *travel arrangements*.

(C) *Postal rates* are not mentioned by either speaker.

**64.** **(A)** The woman tells the man that she *ordered*, or *purchased*, some books *last week*, which is *recently*.

(B) She does not talk about *opening an account*.

(C) She ordered some books, so she is probably expecting to receive some packages, not *send* packages.

(D) She does not mention *London*.

**65.** **(A)** The fact that Ms. Wong says she wants the *university* to be able to spend more on educating *our students* implies that the two women probably work *at a university*.

(B) *A power plant*, (C) *a manufacturing company*, and (D) *a publishing company* are not places where students are educated.

**66.** **(C)** Ms. Wong's proposal is about *cutting down on heating costs*. *Cutting down* means *reducing* and *heating* uses *energy*, so these costs are *energy costs*.

(A) They talk about making changes, but not to *the work schedule*.

(B) The proposal will be presented at a board meeting, but it is not about *appointing new board members*.

(D) Recycling paper is not a way of *reducing energy costs*.

**67.** **(B)** Ms. Wong asks about presenting the ideas in her proposal at the board meeting *next week* and Ms. Sanchez agrees.

The board meeting does not take place (A) *this morning*, (C) *in two weeks*, or (D) *in two months*.

**68.** **(D)** The woman asks about *development of the new coffeemaker* and the speakers talk about preparing it for *a trade show* and *starting an advertising campaign*. Therefore, the conversation is about *a new product*.

(A) They talk about a *trade show in Paris*, not about *a vacation*.

(B) They do not mention *a television show*.

(C) The new product is a *coffeemaker*. They are not talking about a *coffee break*, which is a time allocated for workers to have coffee.

**69.** **(B)** The man talks about having difficulty with the automatic timer, which is a *device* on the coffeemaker.

(A) The man talks about the *advertising* campaign, but he does not mention any *problem* with it.

(C) The *trade show* they speak about has not yet taken place.

(D) They do not refer to *a food delivery*.

**70.** **(D)** The woman mentions *the September trade show*, so we know the trade show will be *in September*.

There is no mention of a trade show (A) *in January*, (B) *in April*, or (C) *in June*.

# PART 4

**71.** **(C)** The woman is leaving a message for Paul. She explains about a problem with her car. She wants to know if Paul could *take a look at it* and asks him to let her know how much it will cost for him to fix it, so she is most likely calling a mechanic.

The woman would not be likely to ask (A) *her supervisor*, (B) *her secretary*, or (D) *a salesperson* to fix her car.

**72.** **(B)** The woman says she thinks *the oil pan in her car is leaking*. She mentions that the oil *is running low* and she finds *oil underneath her car*, which are both signs of an oil leak.

(A) She does not mention a problem with *a broken switch*.

(C) She hopes that Paul *can fit her into his schedule*, but she does not mention *a scheduling conflict*.

(D) She says when she will leave home, but does not mention *a travel delay*.

**73.** **(A)** She asks Paul to *get back to her*, or respond to her request, *soon* and says she will be leaving *in two hours*. Thus, she wants him to respond *within a few hours*, because *a few* means two or three.

She does not request a response (B) *within a day*, (C) *within two days*, or (D) *within* a week.

**74.** **(D)** The key phrases *stay tuned to this station* (radio station) and *now it's time for the weather and traffic report*, indicate that the speaker is a radio announcer.

(A) The speaker is interviewing an actress. He is not *an actor* himself.

(B) He is interviewing the star of a *film*. The speaker is not *a film director*.

(C) The actress will talk about traveling in Australia, but the speaker is not *a travel agent*.

**75.** **(B)** The interview with the actress Maura O'Connor is mainly about her role in the film *Forever and a Day Later*, which the speaker says is *a comedy film*.

The film they will discuss is not (A) *a drama*, (C) *an adventure film*, or (D) *a documentary*.

**76.** **(C)** The speaker says the film premieres in London *on Thursday*, so this is the correct answer.

The London premiere is not (A) *on Tuesday*, (B) *on Wednesday*, or (D) *on Friday*.

**77.** **(A)** The speaker announces that the caller has reached *an account information line* and then gives information about the caller's account, such as *the current balance* and the date *the next payment is due*, so (A) is the correct answer.

(B) The speaker gives some instructions, but the message is not about *mailing instructions*.

(C) The speaker does not give any *hours of operation*.

(D) The message is not about *an order*.

**78.** **(C)** In the message, the speaker says *your next payment is due on January 18*, so (C) is the correct answer.

There is no mention of anything else happening on January 18, so (A), (B), and (D) are incorrect.

**79.** **(D)** The listener is instructed to *press nine* to speak to a customer service representative. In other words, the listener should *select option "nine"*.

(A) The listener is instructed to press a particular number on their phone, not to hang up and *call another number*.

(B) By *staying on the line*, the listener would hear all of the options again, not reach *a customer service representative*.

(C) *Saying the word "zero"* is not mentioned in the message.

**80.** **(A)** At the start of the talk, the speaker announces that they are *entering the laboratory portion of the Alyeska Electronic Piano factory*, so the speaker is in an *electronic piano* or *keyboard factory*.

(B) The speaker is in a factory where they manufacture musical instruments, not at *a concert hall*.

(C) The speaker is entering a laboratory, but it is not *a biology laboratory*.

(D) The factory manufactures electronic pianos. It is not *an electronics store*.

**81.** **(B)** The speaker is discussing research that the company has done and will continue over the next two years to develop electronic keyboards that behave similarly to real pianos.

(A) A future *musical performance* is not mentioned.

(C) The speaker is not discussing the *instructions for operating a machine*.

(D) She talks about the company's emphasis on sound quality, but is not discussing *factory quality inspections*.

**82.** **(C)** Talking about the latest model, the speaker says they *expect to release it in two more years*, which means it will *probably be released in two years*.

She does not indicate that the newest model is likely to be released (A) *in two months* or (B) *in one year*.

(D) They have been developing the latest model for the last *five years*, but they are planning to release it *in two years*.

**83.** **(B)** The speaker discusses changes in *how office waste will be handled*. A *recycling system* is a way of handling waste. The speaker talks about *receptacles for recycling* and says their contents will be sent to a recycling facility.

(A) The speaker does not talk about a *product catalog*.

(C) The speaker is not talking about a *filing plan*.

(D) There is no mention of *an art display*.

84. **(D) The speaker refers to the changes as *starting next Friday* and repeats at the end of the talk that the program *doesn't begin until Friday*, which means it begins *on Friday*.**
   (A) The change in procedure will begin on Friday, not *Tuesday*.
   (B) This is when the recycling containers will be emptied, not when the new system will begin.
   (C) The change in procedure will begin on Friday, not *Thursday*.

85. **(C) The speaker asks the listeners to *take one of the papers as they leave*. *Pick up* means the same as *take* in this context.**
   (A) An office is the context for the announcement, but the audience is not asked *to visit the speaker's office*.
   (B) There is no mention of *ordering items*.
   (D) The recycling receptacles will be in the office, but the listeners are not asked *to reorganize their offices*.

86. **(C) The speaker announces that they must *delay take-off* of *flight 7* and gives instructions for passengers planning to take that flight.**
   (A) The weather in Osaka is mentioned because it is causing the delay, but the *weather in Shanghai* is not described.
   (B) Passengers are not asked to *board the plane*. They are asked to *board a bus*.
   (D) A volunteer *offers* to do something. Here the speaker is informing passengers that they *must* take a later flight.

87. **(B) Meal vouchers will be *distributed*, or given, to the passengers as they board the bus.**
   (A) The speaker does not say passengers will be given *city maps*.
   (C) The airline has arranged transportation by bus from the airport to the hotel and back. The airline will not give the passengers *bus timetables*.
   (D) The speaker does not mention *rail passes*.

88. **(C) Passengers are informed that the bus will leave the hotel at *8 A.M.* the next day.**
   The bus will not leave (A) *at 6 A.M.*, or (B) *at 7 A.M.*
   (D) The flight is scheduled to leave at *10 A.M.*, not the bus.

89. **(C) The company has developed a new *suitcase* model and is conducting a survey to find out how much people are willing to pay for luggage, so the company is *a suitcase manufacturer*.**
   The survey is not being conducted by (A) *a clothing store* or (B) by *a package delivery service*.
   (D) Suitcases are used for traveling, but it is the suitcase manufacturer that is conducting the survey, not *a travel agency*.

90. **(D) Previous surveys have found that people get frustrated when they cannot find things in their suitcases. The speaker says this means they *don't like the way the suitcases are designed*. In other words, they have complained about *poor product design*.**
   (A) The survey being announced is about *price*, but previous surveys looked at other factors.
   (B) The speaker does not mention that customers have complained about *size* in previous surveys.
   (C) *Crowded stores* are not mentioned.

91. **(A) *We've come up with* in the talk means *we've created*. The suitcase model the speaker mentions is *a new product* created by the company.**
   The speaker does not say that the company he works for has created (B) *a Web site*, (C) *a catalog*, or (D) *an instruction manual*.

92. **(A) The speaker is most likely *addressing participants in a training seminar* because she asks the listeners to *pick up a training packet*, talks about *course materials* and *instructors* and announces the first speaker, who will *give a seminar*.**
   (B) The speaker talks *about* the instructors. She is not *addressing* the instructors, which means talking *to* them. Also, this is not *a writing course*.
   (C) *Reporters at a press conference* would not be given training packets and would not be attending a seminar.
   (D) *Visitors to a museum* are not likely to attend a seminar on sales techniques.

93. **(C) The speaker asks the audience members *to pick up a training packet*. The contents of the training packet are *papers*.**
   (A) The speaker does not ask anyone to *leave the room*.
   (B) Audience members are asked to *review a write-up* or read a description of the first speaker, not to *write a report*.
   (D) The speaker asks audience members to familiarize themselves with Mr. Chang's sales techniques by reading the information, not by *introducing themselves* to him.

**94.** **(D)** The speaker asks the participants to read about Mr. Chang's sales techniques before he gives his seminar, so he will probably discuss his *sales techniques*.

    (A) There is no mention of *a recent event* so it is unlikely that Mr. Chang will describe one.

    (B) The audience members are asked to pick up the *course materials* themselves.

    (C) The woman giving this speech is introducing the speaker. Mr. Chang is unlikely to *introduce a speaker*.

**95.** **(A)** The speaker says *we're so happy to have you dining with us*, then describes the *food available* and asks what the listeners would like to *drink*, so he is most likely a waiter.

    (B) The speaker is talking to restaurant customers. He is not *a customer* himself.

    (C) *A chef* does not generally take the customers' orders.

    (D) The speaker is telling the customers about the food available in this restaurant, not talking about food on a radio program.

**96.** **(D)** The speaker describes the vegetables as *purchased fresh from local farmers*, which implies *they are locally grown*.

    (A) *Steaming* is a way of cooking vegetables. The speaker does not say how the vegetables are cooked.

    (B) The speaker does not mention the *price of the vegetables*.

    (C) Since he is recommending the vegetables, they must be available.

**97.** **(A)** At the end of the talk, the speaker asks what he can get the customers to drink. A *beverage* is a drink, so he asks for the customers' *beverage order*.

    (B) A waiter does not ask for *a bill*.

    (C) A waiter does not ask for *a restaurant menu*.

    (D) *A recipe* gives instructions for cooking a dish. A waiter does not need a recipe.

**98.** **(B)** The speaker says she wants to see *the types of photos* Ms. Dai has taken, so Ms. Dai is most likely a photographer.

    (A) There is no mention of advertising or selling advertising, so Ms. Dai is not likely to be *an advertising salesperson*.

    (C) The speaker does not say Ms. Dai has worked as *a receptionist*.

    (D) The speaker mentions work Ms. Dai has done for a magazine, but she does not describe it as *writing*.

**99.** **(A)** The speaker asks Ms. Dai to bring *a portfolio of her work*, which is a collection of samples of her work.

    (B) The speaker refers to *the list of references* Ms. Dai has already sent her, so she does not ask Ms. Dai to bring this with her.

    (C) The speaker has also already received *a résumé*.

    (D) A job applicant sends *a cover letter* with a job application and the speaker says she has already received that.

**100.** **(D)** The speaker would like to schedule the interview for Friday, so it is most likely that it will take place *on Friday*.

    (A) Monday is the day when the speaker received the application. She does not suggest holding the interview on a *Monday*.
    She does not ask to schedule the interview on (B) *Wednesday* or (C) *Thursday*, so it is not likely to take place on either of those days.

# PART 5

**101.** **(C)** The present perfect tense *has transferred* is needed because Ms. Walters' move happened at an unspecified time in the past, but has an effect in the present.

    (A) The simple present tense *transfer* cannot be used here because the action happened in the past.

    (B) The gerund *transferring* is incorrect because a verb tense is needed here.

    (D) The adjective *transferable* is incorrect as a verb is needed to describe the action of Ms. Walters.

**102.** **(C)** The preposition *from* is used here to talk about the origin of something, in this case the desserts.

    (A) *With* shows that one thing accompanies another, for example when we say "I'd like chocolate sauce *with* my ice-cream." That is not the case here.

    (B) *By* is used to indicate who or what performed an action. *Regions of the world* did not perform an action here.

    (D) *Until* is a preposition of time. A preposition of space is needed here.

**103.** **(B)** The demonstrative pronoun *those* should be used here to mean *any people*.

    (A) *These* is incorrect here because it is used to refer to particular people.

    (C) *This* is a singular pronoun and is used to refer to a particular thing or person, so it is incorrect here.

    (D) *That* is singular. The sentence is directed at more than one person.

104. **(D)** *Trend* **should be used for a change in the type of ingredients used in cosmetics. Using the adjective** *growing* **with the noun** *trend* **is an acceptable collocation; that is, these words are often used together.**

A growing (A) *product*, (B) *scent*, and (C) *sale* are not words that are used together, so these choices are incorrect.

105. **(A)** **An adjective to describe melodies or tunes is needed. Melodies can be described as** *simple*.

(B) *Patient* and (C) *kind* are adjectives which describe people, so they are incorrect.

(D) The adjective *blank* means *having nothing written or recorded on it*. It is not used to describe *melodies*.

106. **(A)** **An adverb is needed after the verb. The adverb** *responsibly* **describes how visitors are expected to behave.**

(B) The adjective *responsible* cannot be used to describe the verb.

(C) *Responsibility* and (D) *Responsibilities* are nouns. A noun is not used after the verb *behave*.

107. **(D)** **We use the conjunction** *or* **to link two or more things in a sentence containing** *not* **or another word with negative meaning.**

(A) *Yet* can be a conjunction meaning *nevertheless* and is generally used to introduce a verb clause. *Overtime pay to part-time employees* is not a verb clause, so *yet* is incorrect.

(B) *If* also introduces a verb clause, so it is not correct here.

(C) The conjunction *but* is used to show contrast. *Sick leave* and *overtime pay* are not contrasting ideas here. They are both benefits given by an employer.

108. **(A)** **The noun** *election* **is needed with the definite article** *the*.

(B) *Elected* is the past participle of *elect*. A noun is needed here, not a verb.

(C) *Elects* is also a verb, so it is incorrect.

(D) *Electable* is an adjective, so it is not correct here.

109. **(B)** *Sold*, **the past participle of** *sell*, **forms a participle clause with the words** *by American publishers* **to describe** *new university-level textbooks*.

(A) *Priced* would need to be followed by an actual price e.g. *priced at less than $40,* so it is incorrect.

(C) *Marked* would not form a meaningful participle clause with *by American publishers*.

(D) Students are *instructed* by books. *Instructed* cannot be used to describe textbooks.

110. **(D)** **The comparative adjective** *worse* **should be used to complete the comparison** *worse than usual*, **describing** *traffic congestion*.

(A) An adjective is needed, not an adverb.

(B) The adjective *bad* is incorrect because it is not the comparative form of the adjective.

(C) *Worst* is the superlative form of *bad*, so it is incorrect.

111. **(D)** **An adverb can be used before** *sell off* **to comment on the investors' action of selling off their stocks.** *Typically* **here means generally or usually.**

The adverbs (A) *exactly*, (B) *greatly*, and (C) *approximately* cannot be used to describe *sell off*.

112. **(A)** **The verb following** *expect* **should be a verb infinitive with** *to*, **so** *buy* **is correct here.**

(B) This is incorrect because *buying* is a gerund, not an infinitive.

(C) *Bought* is the simple past form of the verb *to buy*, not the infinitive.

(D) The present perfect *has bought* is also incorrect.

113. **(A)** *Proposal* **is the correct noun to use with** *marketing*. **A** *marketing proposal* **is a plan for marketing or promoting something, in this case tourism in a particular region.**

(B) We do not generally use *permission* with marketing. Also, *permission* is not something that can be developed.

(C) An *appliance* is a piece of equipment. We do not talk about a *marketing appliance*.

(D) We do not use *employment* with *marketing*, so this choice is incorrect.

114. **(B)** **A** *manner of speaking* **is a person's way of speaking. A person who has a** *direct manner of speaking* **generally says exactly what they mean.**

(A) *Mutual* means *shared by more than one person*, so it cannot be used for a single person, the Prime Minister.

(C) *Adjacent* means *next to*, so it cannot describe someone's *manner of speaking*.

(D) *Existing* cannot be modified by *very* and cannot describe *manner of speaking*.

115. **(D)** **A relative pronoun which refers to a person,** *Henri Valois*, **is needed, so** *who* **is the correct choice.**

(A) The relative pronoun *that* can be used for a person, but only in a defining relative clause. Here, the relative clause after the comma is a non-defining relative clause.

(B) *It* is not a relative pronoun and also refers to a thing, not a person.

(C) The relative pronoun *which* cannot be used to refer to a person.

116. **(C)** **The adverb *correctly* should be used here to talk about the manner of applying the products. The adverb *correctly* modifies the verb *apply*.** Neither (A) *correction*, which is a noun, nor (B) *corrected*, a past participle, nor (D) *correcting*, a verb gerund, can be used to modify *apply*.

117. **(A)** **The conjunction *since* should be used to introduce the clause containing the verb *was released*. The verb in the main clause, in this case *has not published*, is often in the present perfect tense.**
    - (B) *Under* is used when a book is published using a different name from that of the author e.g. *This book was published under the name of Gerald Green*. That is not the case here.
    - (C) *Between* can be used as a time preposition, but two points in time have to be mentioned.
    - (D) *During* is a time preposition and so it cannot be used to introduce the clause containing the verb *was released*.

118. **(D)** **A noun is needed after *her* as the grammatical object of the verb *will use*. *Using your discretion* means using your own judgment to decide what to do in a particular situation.**
    - (A) *Discretionary* is an adjective, not a noun.
    - (B) *Discrete* is also an adjective, not a noun.
    - (C) *Discretely* is an adverb, not a noun.

119. **(B)** **A verb is required to describe the process of changing ideas into well-executed projects. *To transform* means to change. It has an object, followed by *into*.**
    - (A) *To prevail* means that something commonly exists. It does not need an object and is not used with *into*.
    - (C) *To inspire* means to *give somebody an idea*. It is not used with the preposition into.
    - (D) *Involve* has the preposition *in* after its object, not *into* e.g. *Many researchers were involved in the development of the new product*.

120. **(A)** **The past participle *delighted* should be used to complete the clause at the beginning of the sentence and give the meaning *Because the band was delighted by...*.**
    - (B) The adverb *delightedly* cannot be used with *by* to describe the effect the audience's reaction had on the band.
    - (C) The adjective *delightful* can be used to describe music, but cannot be used with *by* and a noun.
    - (D) *Delight* is a noun. A noun is incorrect here.

121. **(C)** ***Whether* should be used with *or* as a double conjunction to mean that the advice *to use a real estate agent* is true in both situations, buying and selling a house.**
    - (A) The preposition *until* is incorrect because it would mean that you should only use a real estate agent up to the point of buying or selling a house. A real estate agent is in fact used throughout the transaction.
    - (B) *Mainly* is an adverb, so it is incorrect here.
    - (D) *Only* can be an adverb or adjective, so it is not the correct part of speech to use here.

122. **(D)** **The adverb *ever* should be used, meaning *at any other time*. The phrase *easier than ever* is used to compare the new application process with previous processes.**
    - (A) *Once* cannot be used alone to complete the comparison here. The phrase would have to be *easier than it once was*.
    - (B) The negative *never* meaning *not ever* is not correct here.
    - (C) *Not* cannot be used to complete the comparison here.

123. **(D)** **Certain adverbs can be used to modify the adjective *small*. The adverb *relatively*, which means *fairly* is suitable here.** The adverbs (A) *nearly*, (B) *closely*, and (C) *precisely* cannot be used to modify *small*, so none of these choices is correct.

124. **(C)** **The adjective *significant* can be used to describe the growth of a company. It means *quite large*.**
    - (A) *Chief* means *main* or *most important*. It is not used to describe *growth*.
    - (B) *Prior* is an adjective meaning *previous*. This meaning is not appropriate here.
    - (D) We say the figures relating to a company's growth are *official* if they are verified by an accountant, but *growth* cannot be official.

125. **(B)** **The sentence is probably about a publication such as a magazine or newspaper. When readers give their opinion of a publication, it is called *feedback*, and we talk about *positive* and negative feedback.**
    - (A) An *inquiry* cannot be described as *positive*.
    - (C) An *intention* is something a person plans to do. The sentence does not refer to a plan.
    - (D) *Hesitation* would not be used with the preposition *from* and would not be described as *positive*.

126. **(A) The words *one another* are needed to make the phrase, *fairly close to one another*, which means that each house is quite close to the next one.**
(B) *another* and (C) *the other* cannot be used to refer to several houses, so they are incorrect.
(D) The word *other* is grammatically incorrect here because it would need to be followed by *houses* or it would need to be in the plural, which is *others*.

127. **(D) The adverb *recognizably* can be used to modify the adjective *different*.**
The three other choices are incorrect because (A) is a verb, (B) is a verb gerund, and (C) is an adjective and none of these can be used to modify an adjective.

128. **(C) *For* is the dependent preposition used with *recommend* to indicate the purpose or situation for which something is considered useful.**
(A) The preposition *as* is sometimes used with *recommend*, but then it is used to indicate the role in which something might be useful e.g. "I recommend this hotel as a conference venue since it has all the necessary facilities".
(B) and (D) are incorrect because a preposition is needed with *recommend*.

129. **(B) The adverb *promptly* should be used to say that the reports should be delivered *punctually*.**
(A) The adverb *recently* is used for something that happened a short time ago in the past, so it is not correct here.
(C) *Formerly* also refers to the past because it means *before now*.
(D) *Briefly* cannot describe the manner of delivering something.

130. **(B) A noun is needed after *their* as the grammatical object of the verb *reduce*. *Dependence* is a noun.**
(A) The adverb *dependently*, (C) the adjective *dependent*, and (D) the verb *depend* are incorrect after *their*.

131. **(B) The preposition *among* can be used with the plural noun *achievements* to mean *one of* the firm's achievements.**
(A) *Into* is not used to mean *one of several*.
(C) *Despite* is incorrect here because it expresses contrast, which is not intended here, and it does not fit with the structure of the sentence.
(D) *Around* does not mean *one of several*.

132. **(D) An adjective which can describe a notion, or idea, should be used here. *Foolish*, which means *unwise*, is a suitable adjective.**
A notion is not generally described as (A) *mobile*, (B) *talkative*, or (C) *dedicated*.

133. **(A) *Conducted*, the past participle of the verb *conduct*, should be used with *by the Fielding Institute* to describe the survey.**
(B) The noun *conductor* cannot be used here.
(C) The present participle *conducting* is incorrect because it has an active meaning. A past participle is needed here because it has a passive meaning.
(D) The simple present tense *conducts* is incorrect. A past participle is needed.

134. **(C) The adverb *comprehensibly* should be used to modify the verb *to express*, saying how the ideas should be expressed.**
An adverb is needed here, not (A) the verb *comprehend*, (B) the adjective *comprehensible*, or (D) the noun *comprehensibility*.

135. **(A) The conjunction *when* should be used before *authorized by the client* to describe the conditions that must exist for the higher rate of pay to be received.**
(B) *As if* cannot be used to introduce a conditional clause.
(C) *So that* is used to introduce a clause describing purpose, not a conditional clause.
(D) *Than* is used in a comparison. No comparison is made here.

136. **(A) The adjective *frustrating* is needed to describe the noun *drawback*. *Frustrating* means *causing frustration*.**
(B) *Frustratingly* is an adverb, not an adjective.
(C) *Frustrated* has a passive meaning and would be used to describe the way the reader feels, not a drawback of the book.
(D) *Frustration* is a noun, not an adjective.

137. **(C) The Sagamore brothers are evidently tailors. The word *creating* fits best with the object *custom-made shirts*, forming the present perfect continuous tense of the verb.**
(A) *Assigning* would not be used to describe the work the brothers have been doing in their workshop.
(B) The work of tailors is not to calculate shirts, so *calculating* is incorrect.
(D) *Describing* is not the main work carried out by tailors in a workshop.

138. **(B)** **Before a project is carried out it is necessary to investigate, or *analyze*, the *feasibility* of it; that is, determine whether the project is possible and achievable.**
- (A) We do not talk about analyzing the *uncertainty* of a project.
- (C) The noun *quantity* cannot be used before *of removing dams*.
- (D) The noun *flexibility* does not fit with *of removing dams*.

139. **(A)** **The adverb *well* can be used to modify *attended*. If an event is *well attended* it means many people attended it.**
- (B) *Quite* is not used with *attended*, though we do say *quite well attended*.
- (C) The adverb *well* is needed, not the adjective *many*.
- (D) The determiner *some* cannot be used with *attended*.

140. **(D)** **The adverb *already* should be used here to describe the adjective *inflated*. *Already* indicates that the market became inflated even before customers moved to the Web-based marketplace.**
- (A) *Even*, (B) *else*, and (C) *urgently* cannot be used to describe *inflated market*.

## PART 6

141. **(D)** **The memo, dated July 11, states that the change in prices *took effect*, or started, on May 1. The present perfect tense should be used for increase because it links the past, when the increase was introduced, with the present, when it is still effective.**
- (A) *Are to increase* is used for something that is planned for the future.
- (B) *Would have increased* is used in a past conditional sentence. This is not a conditional sentence. It is clear that the increase has happened.
- (C) *Will increase* is a future tense, so is incorrect here.

142. **(C)** **Companies often have special phone numbers which allow customers to call the company without paying for the call. The noun *charge*, meaning payment, is required after *no*.**
- (A) This sentence is about an action by the company, not by a customer. A *complaint* is usually made by a customer, so *complaint* is incorrect.
- (B) *Record* does not refer to a payment and is followed by *of*.
- (D) *Value* cannot be used to mean the payment made for a call.

143. **(B)** **An adjective should be used to describe the noun *service*. Here two adjectives, *quick* and *courteous*, meaning polite are used.**
- (A) *Courtesy* is a noun, so it is not correct here.
- (C) The adverb *courteously* is not correct here.
- (D) The noun *courteousness* is not correct here.

144. **(C)** **Like the other verbs in the first paragraph, *choose* should be in the passive voice, to describe something that happened to Dr. Lew. *Were chosen* is simple past passive.**
- (A) The future active *will choose* is incorrect because the sentence is not about something Dr. Lew and the others on the list will do themselves.
- (B) *Are choosing* refers to something happening now and is in the active voice, so it is incorrect.
- (D) *Been chosen* is incorrect because it is not simple past tense.

145. **(B)** **The plural possessive pronoun *their* is needed here to refer to the *contributions of the candidates*.**
- (A) The reflexive pronoun *themselves* is incorrect because it does not show possession.
- (C) The pronoun *theirs* is not used directly before a noun.
- (D) The pronoun *them* does not show possession and is used in place of a noun, not before a noun.

146. **(A)** **The noun *honor*, meaning special recognition, should be used here because being included in the list described is a way of recognizing a person's special achievements.**
- (B) *Amount* would refer to money. There is no mention of money here.
- (C) *Salary* also refers to money, so it is incorrect.
- (D) Dr. Lew may feel *pride* at receiving this honor, but we do not say she is *given* pride.

147. **(B)** **The memo says the repainting of the apartment buildings will begin on April 16. The preposition *before* should be used here to make it clear when objects should be removed.**
- (A) Objects should be removed from windows and balconies to avoid interfering with the repainting. It would not make sense to remove them *after* the painting has been done.
- (C) *Until* does not fit logically with *remove all objects*.
- (D) *Since* indicates the point in the past when an action began. The memo is not about the past.

148. **(A)** ***Also* should be used here to introduce a second point in the memo.**
- (B) *Once* cannot be used before *be cautious* and a person would not be advised to *be cautious once*.
- (C) The adverb *nearly* is not used with *be cautious*.
- (D) *Soon* would be unnecessary because *during this time* makes it clear when people should *be cautious*.

**149. (A)** The adjective *pleased* should be used to modify *you*, meaning the residents. It describes the way the manager hopes the residents will feel.
- (B) *Pleasing* would be used to describe the results, not the feelings of the residents.
- (C) *Pleasant* would not be used to describe the feelings of the residents.
- (D) The adverb *pleasantly* cannot be used to modify the pronoun *you*.

**150. (D)** The verb *serve* should be used here to say that the *technology instruction centers* will be useful to residents.
- (A) The centers will *conduct classes*, but *conduct* cannot be used with the object *residents*.
- (B) *Determine* means to decide something. It cannot be used with *residents* here.
- (C) The centers will not *house*, which means *provide accommodation for*, residents.

**151. (C)** A noun referring to a person is needed with the adjective *full-time*. A *director* is the person in charge of an educational institution.
- (A) *Direct* is a verb or adjective. A noun is needed here.
- (B) *Directed* is the past participle of the verb.
- (D) The word *direction* is a noun, but it does not refer to a person.

**152. (A)** Ms. Vali applied for a grant and the letter announces that her organization has been awarded the grant, so her application has been *successful*.
- (B) *Pending* is incorrect because it means the application has not yet been considered.
- (C) A *conditional* application would be one that has not actually been made.
- (D) The letter does not say the application had been submitted once and then *revised*, so (D) is not correct.

# PART 7

**153. (B)** The company is advertising a *service to create a customized*, or specially designed space from *an unused room*. This is a *design service* carried out by the company's *design team*.
- (A) The company does not offer *rooms to rent*, it designs rooms.
- (C) A *job placement service* to help people find jobs is not being advertised.
- (D) *Vacation packages* are not being advertised.

**154. (C)** People are invited to call to arrange a *free initial consultation*.
- (A) There is no mention of *free exercise equipment*.
- (B) The company's free brochure gives a *sampling* of options for room designs. *Paint samples* are not mentioned.
- (D) A *plan* for the room would probably be made, but a free *architectural plan* is not being offered.

**155. (B)** The letter states that the recipient's magazine subscription ends soon and mentions the advantages of renewing the subscription, so the purpose is to *encourage subscription renewal*.
- (A) The recipient already has a subscription to *Theater Digest*, so it is not *a new publication*.
- (C) No *billing error* is mentioned.
- (D) The letter is not a request for a *donation*, or gift of money.

**156. (A)** The letter states that by renewing the subscription the subscriber will continue to receive *Theater Digest every month*, so it is published *once a month*.
- (B) The subscription will end *in two months*, but the magazine is not published *every two months*. *Theater Digest* is not published (C) *twice a year* or (D) *once a year*.

**157. (C)** The letter suggests visiting the Web site to read about *contests* for readers, which are *competitions*.
- (A) The letter does not mention *access to other theater-related Web sites*.
- (B) The letter only mentions that the Web site has information about *contests for readers*.
- (D) There is no mention of making *online payments* via the Web site.

**158. (B)** The information is about transportation to the NACU Conference for conference attendees, so it would most likely be found on the Web site of *NACU*.

This information is intended for conference attendees, not the general public, so it is unlikely to be found on the Web site of (A) *Sky High Air*, (C) *Regency Hotel*, or (D) *Airporter*.

159. **(B)** **In this context, *serve* is closest in meaning to *operate*. Particular airlines often agree to operate as the official carriers for attendees to a large conference.**
  (A) In the context of food service in a restaurant, *serve* means *wait on*, but this information is not about a restaurant.
  (C) *Serve* can mean to work for a person and in that context it can mean *obey*, but that is not the meaning here.
  (D) *Give out* means distribute. That is not the correct meaning here.

160. **(D)** **In the section on Ground Transportation the information says this journey will take *45 minutes by car*.**
  The information does not say it will take (A) *15 minutes*, (B) *20 minutes*, or (C) *30 minutes*.

161. **(C)** **It costs *$10.00* to park at the Regency Hotel on Thursdays because the information says this is the price *per day Monday to Friday*.**
  (A) It costs *$6.00* on Sunday, not on *Thursdays*.
  (B) It costs *$8.00* on Saturday, not on *Thursdays*.
  (D *$15.00* is the fee for parking at the Fairmont Hotel, not at the *Regency Hotel*.

162. **(B)** **The information is about prices for placing advertisements in the *Ridgeway Herald News*, so it is intended for *advertisers*.**
  (A) An editor may work for a newspaper, but this information is not intended for *editors*.
  (C) *Photographers* do not usually place the advertisements in a publication, so this information is not intended for them.
  (D) There is nothing to indicate the information is intended for *lawyers*.

163. **(D)** ***Picture* is another word for *photo*. The information states that *one photo is included in the price*, so *a picture may be submitted*.**
  (A) Payment should be submitted with the advertisement *before publication*, not *after publication*.
  (B) The information is only about black and white advertisements.
  (C) No policy relating to *a late fee* is given.

164. **(C)** **The letter invites Mr. Adams to a special evening to celebrate Toppo Travel's twentieth year, in other words *an anniversary celebration*.**
  (A) The event will be *held at a hotel*, but it is not the *grand opening of a hotel*.
  (B) The event is not *a retirement dinner*. There is no mention of anybody retiring.
  (D) The event is not *an awards ceremony*.

165. **(A)** **According to the letter, Mr. Adams became a customer of Toppo *five years ago*, so he has been traveling with them *for five years*.**
  He has not been traveling with the company for (B) *six years*, (C) *ten years*, or (D) *twenty years*.

166. **(C)** **The event features *exotic fare*, which means *exotic food* and the letter describes the *buffet*, a meal where people serve themselves from a selection of food.**
  (A) There is no mention of *a slide show*.
  (B) The event will be in the Grand Ballroom of the hotel, but *ballroom dancing* is not mentioned.
  (D) There is no mention of any *speaker*.

167. **(C)** **The notice gives *guidelines*, or *rules* for recycling products and is for residents, so it is about recycling *household* items.**
  (A) The notice says garbage pick-up will continue *according to the regular schedule*, so *a revised schedule for garbage collection* is not announced.
  (B) *Fees* for collecting garbage are not mentioned.
  (D) The notice is about a *new recycling program*, not a *new recycling center*.

168. **(A)** **The information states that the *green plastic bins*, or *containers*, will be *provided by the city* and delivered in a particular week, so *city employees will supply them*.**
  It is the city who will supply the green containers, not (B) *bottling company staff*, (C) *recycling center volunteers*, or (D) *Alder Park residents*.

169. **(B)** **Papers for recycling should be put in the green plastic bins. They will be picked up *during the first and third weeks of each month*, which is *two times per month*.**
  They will not be picked up (A) *one time per month*, (C) *three times per month*, or (D) *four times per month*.

170. **(B)** **In the "Notes" column related to glass, the information states *No broken glass*, so bottles *should not be broken*.**
  (A) The notice does not state that bottles should be *wrapped in newspaper*, though newspapers can be put in the green bins.
  (C) Bottles will be collected *twice a month* with all the other items in the green bins.
  (D) According to the notice *labels are permitted*, so (D) is incorrect.

171. **(D) A flaw has been found in Lasell's 6000X model vacuum cleaner. The purpose of the letter is to inform customers that they can return the product and receive a new one, which is *a replacement plan*.**
    (A) The first two paragraphs outline the company's policy regarding any flaws in their products. The letter does not *introduce a policy change*.
    (B) No *invitation to an in-store event* is given.
    (C) The letter is not *a response to a customer complaint*. The problem was found by the company itself.

172. **(D) The customer is asked to contact, probably by phone, their nearest Lasell store and the store will then arrange for the machine to be picked up. Thus, the reader should *call to schedule a pick-up*.**
    (A) The reader should arrange to have the machine picked up. This can be done even if there is not actually *a problem* with it.
    (B) A free gift is offered if a customer exchanges their machine, but there is no mention of picking it up in the office.
    (C) The customer is not told to send or *submit a copy of the receipt*.

173. **(A) The mention of Lasell's *product testing* program and *quality assurance team* indicate that it is a manufacturer. The product the letter is about is a vacuum cleaner, which is a household *appliance*.**
    (B) Lasell wants to ensure the safety of its products, but *safety assessment* is not its main area of business.
    (C) Lasell does not produce *packaging materials*.
    (D) This is not a delivery company making *commercial deliveries*.

174. **(A) In the *responsibilities* section it is stated that the person who gets the job of *brand manager* will be working in the *marketing* sector of the company's *International Division*, so will be working in *International marketing*.**
    (B) *Human resources* deals with hiring new employees. The successful applicant will not work in this division.
    (C) The successful applicant will market the products, not work *in production*.
    (D) The successful applicant will not be in *the accounting division*.

175. **(C) Increasing product recognition *domestically*, or nationally, is NOT stated as a job responsibility. The role is to *heighten product recognition abroad*.**
    (A) A stated responsibility is to *generate marketing plans*. *Generate* means the same as *create*.
    (B) One responsibility is to *evaluate market requirements and opportunities*.
    (D) A stated responsibility is to work *with sales operations departments*, which involves *working with sales representatives*.

176. **(D) In a marketing context to *foster* growth means to *encourage* growth. The phrases *build brand recognition* and *increase public awareness of products* provide clues to the meaning of *foster*.**
    (A) *Substitute* means *exchange* one thing for another, which is not the meaning of *foster*.
    (B) The brand manager may *measure* growth in a product, but *foster* does not mean *measure*.
    (C) *Foster* can mean *cherish* in the context of looking after children, but that is not the meaning here.

177. **(D) *Strong experience in analyzing current markets* is given as a qualification of the ideal candidate, so the successful application will possess *experience in market analysis*.**
    (A) The company produces some products related to home improvement, but *experience in the home improvement industry* is not a requirement.
    (B) A degree in *marketing* is required, not a degree in *finance*.
    (C) There is no mention of *fluency in a foreign language* being required.

178. **(C) The announcement talks about sending confirmation to applicants *via e-mail*, which means Juneco will contact them *by e-mail*.** Applicants will not be contacted (A) *by phone*, (B) *by fax*, or (D) *by mail*.

179. **(C) A special offer for customers who subscribe before July 30 is detailed in the last paragraph. The price of three months of offline storage will be *just under $120*.**
    (A) *$39.95* is the price for one month of *online* storage.
    (B) *$59.95* is the regular cost of *one month* of offline storage.
    (D) *$180* is the *regular* cost of three months of offline storage, but customers who join before July 30 will get a special price.

180. **(A)** *Technical support* **is one of the company's services to customers, but is NOT mentioned as a feature of** *TDM News*.

(B) Reviews, or *discussions* of computer equipment are given in *TDM News*.

(C) Ratings and reviews of new software, in other words *assessments*, are given in *TDM News*.

(D) *TDM News* has a *help wanted section*, which would include *job opportunities for computer technicians*.

181. **(D)** **The letter announces** *a drawing* **to raise money for the theater. This is a type of** *fund-raising event*. **If a person donates $20 to the theater their name will be entered in the drawing once. On May 20 a name will be selected, or drawn, and this is the name of the prize winner.**

(A) The letter is not *an invitation to an event*.

(B) The letter does not *advertise a new show*.

(C) The letter was not written *to explain a new ticketing policy*.

182. **(C)** **Ms. Kessler is writing on behalf of the Blixen Memorial Theater and she writes** *we hold a drawing every year*, **so the theater holds an** *annual drawing*.

(A) Ms. Kessler does not say the theater *has had to reduce its budget*.

(B) The drawing takes place on May 20. This is not the date of the beginning of the new season.

(D) She does not say the theater is *offering discount tickets* to people who give money.

183. **(B)** **The prize is four tickets for each theater performance in the upcoming year, in other words** *a year's worth of theater tickets*.

(A) The value of the tickets which are the prize is $3,000. The prize is not *a check for $3,000*.

(C) The prize tickets are for *ten* performances, not *four*, and *seat location* is not mentioned.

(D) The prize is not to *meet performers after the shows*.

184. **(A)** **In this context,** *present* **means** *in attendance*. *The winner need not be present* **implies that a person could win free tickets without being at the drawing.**

(B) When talking about time, *present* can mean *current*, but this information is not about time, but about attending performances.

(C) *Present* is not close in meaning to *on hold*, which is a phrase used to describe somebody waiting on the phone.

(D) The letter is from a theater, but *present* does not mean *performing*.

185. **(B)** **The form Anton Maldonado has completed is the entry form for the drawing mentioned in the letter. He asks for his credit card to be charged $40, so he** *will contribute* **$40 to the theater.**

(A) This is not a form for *purchasing tickets* because at the bottom the form says *Attention: Raffle*. *Raffle* is another word for *drawing*.

(C) He has not completed the section for paying by check.

(D) He is not requesting a schedule.

186. **(B)** **Mike O'Malley sent the e-mail to Scott Abernathy to ask for** *a change* **in the delivery date and where part of the order should be sent.**

(A) Mike did not ask *to cancel the shipment*, he only requested changes.

(C) Mike did not *invite Scott to the factory*.

(D) The e-mail is about an order for lamp parts. It is not *a furniture order*.

187. **(C)** **Saturday must be the day Vincent Balasco will visit the showroom because Scott wishes Mike luck with** *showing the lamps on Saturday*. **This refers back to Mike's mention of the visit in his e-mail.**

The visit will not take place on (A) *Thursday*, (B) *Friday*, or (D) *Sunday*.

188. **(A)** **In the e-mail, Mike says that the reason for delivering the shades at the showroom instead of the warehouse is to show them to Vincent Balasco there, who is** *a potential buyer*.

(B) The shipping order shows that much of the order is still being sent to the Industry Road Warehouse. There is no mention of it being *closed*.

(C) The *distance* from the Zenith warehouse to the showroom is not the reason for sending the order to two different places.

(D) Mike O'Malley is not *opening a second showroom*.

189. **(B)** **When he mentions Vincent Balasco, Mike says he could become a supplier for** *his furniture stores*. **His refers to Vincent Balasco, so Vincent Balasco must be a furniture store owner.**

The information given about Vincent Balasco shows he cannot be (A) *a warehouse clerk*, (C) *a lamp shade manufacturer*, or (D) *a truck driver*.

190. **(D)** **$1,460 is given on the shipping order as the total cost of the merchandise; that is, everything Mike O'Malley has purchased.**

The total cost is not (A) *$360*, (B) *$500*, or (C) *$600*.

**191.** **(A)** *Experience working in a hospital* is NOT stated as a requirement for the volunteer positions announced.
  (B) A *recommendation* from an employer is a requirement. The recommendation would probably be in a letter.
  (C) *Completion of training* is mandatory, which means it must be done.
  (D) The announcement gives *a commitment to one shift per week* as a requirement.

**192.** **(A)** At the end of the announcement, *May 15* is given as *the deadline* for applications for the summer. A deadline is the date something is due.
  (B) *May 17* is the date Josh sent in his application, which was *after* the due date.
  (C) *May 21* is not the date applications are due.
  (D) *May 22* is the date of the orientation, not the due date for applications.

**193.** **(D)** Josh apologizes for his late application and explains the reason for it. This is an implied *request for special consideration*.
  (A) Josh has attached all the documents required in the announcement, so he does not need *more time to obtain a recommendation letter*.
  (B) He does not ask to work *in the hospital restaurant*.
  (C) He says *he will be able to attend the orientation*, so he is not asking for *permission to miss this*.

**194.** **(B)** In his e-mail Josh is applying for the summer session and says he wants to volunteer on Tuesdays. The announcement states that summer shifts Monday through Friday are six hours long, so he is volunteering for *six hours*.
  (A) Work shifts are *four hours* on Saturdays and Sundays, not *Tuesdays*.
  None of the shifts for volunteers are (C) *eight hours* or (D) *ten hours* long.

**195.** **(C)** The word *restricted* is closest in meaning to *limited*. Josh explains that he has a restaurant job on Saturdays and Sundays which will *restrict* his availability.
  (A) *Limited* does not mean *unavailable* here.
  (B) *Adequate* means that a person has enough time to do something. This is not the meaning of *limited*.
  (D) *Shared* does not mean *limited*, so this is not the correct choice.

**196.** **(B)** The article states that the trains currently in service were introduced *25 years ago*, so they have been *in service 25 years*.
  (A) *30 years* is given as the life expectancy of the current trains, not the time they have been *in service*.
  (C) The current trains have not been *in service for 14 years*.
  (D) *3 years* is the time within which all the current trains will be taken out of service, not the time they have been *in service*.

**197.** **(B)** According to the article, company officials, or *executives*, were very *excited by the performance of the new trains*, so they were *impressed*. Because of this, the new trains will be introduced in three years, not five years.
  (A) The article does not mention letters *from passengers to government officials*.
  (C) There is no mention of *reduced rates from the manufacturer*.
  (D) *A population increase* is not given as a reason for moving up the schedule.

**198.** **(A)** According to the article, there were long talks with the government because the government *was reluctant to*, or did not want to, help fund the project. The railway spokesperson implies that the government thought buying the new trains would be *too expensive*.
  (B) No problem with *finalizing the design* is mentioned.
  (C) The article does not mention the appointment of a new president.
  (D) There is no mention of *a power supply problem*.

**199.** **(B)** Mr. O'Farrel says the government realized an adequate transportation system was *indispensable for the continued development and prosperity of the region*. *Indispensable for* means *essential for*, so he implies that good transportation will *help the region's economic growth*.
  (A) Mr. O'Farrel does not imply that the region's economic growth will be *difficult to sustain*.
  (C) He does not talk about *the pace* at which the region's economy will grow.
  (D) Mr. O'Farrel does not imply that *foreign investment* is needed to help the region's economy grow.

**200.** **(B)** The article states that GR will upgrade the longest routes first. From the table, it can be seen that the *Weston to Barlow* route, at 162 kilometers, is the longest.
  The other three routes shown in the table are shorter than Weston to Barlow, so (A), (C), and (D) are incorrect.

# Practice Test 1: Quick Check Answer Key

## Listening Test

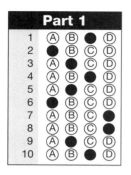
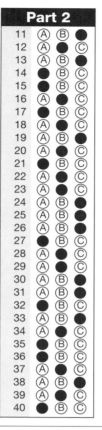
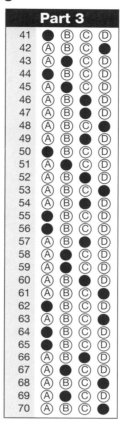
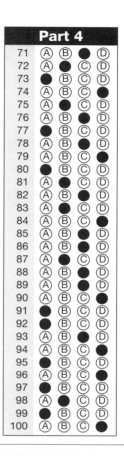

**Part 1** | **Part 2** | **Part 3** | **Part 4**

## Reading Test

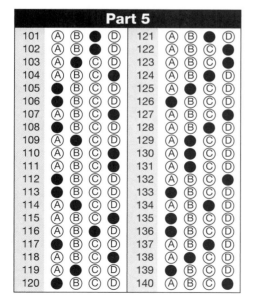
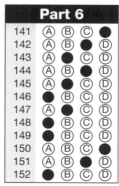
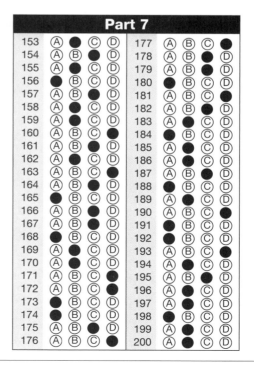

**Part 5** | **Part 6** | **Part 7**

# Tactics for TOEIC® Listening and Reading Test Score Conversion Tables

### Getting an estimated TOEIC score

Compare the total number of correct answers (raw score) in each of the listening and reading sections of the test to the appropriate section of the tables below.
Add the converted listening and reading scores together to get an estimated total score.

| Listening Raw Score | Listening Scaled Score | Reading Raw Score | Reading Scaled Score |
|---|---|---|---|
| 96–100 | 495 | 96–100 | 470–495 |
| 91–95 | 450–495 | 91–95 | 430–475 |
| 86–90 | 415–475 | 86–90 | 405–440 |
| 81–85 | 370–450 | 81–85 | 375–420 |
| 76–80 | 340–420 | 76–80 | 350–395 |
| 71–75 | 315–390 | 71–75 | 325–380 |
| 66–70 | 285–360 | 66–70 | 295–350 |
| 61–65 | 255–330 | 61–65 | 265–325 |
| 56–60 | 230–305 | 56–60 | 235–295 |
| 51–55 | 205–275 | 51–55 | 205–270 |
| 46–50 | 175–245 | 46–50 | 170–235 |
| 41–45 | 150–220 | 41–45 | 140–205 |
| 36–40 | 125–185 | 36–40 | 110–175 |
| 31–35 | 100–155 | 31–35 | 90–145 |
| 26–30 | 85–120 | 26–30 | 70–120 |
| 21–25 | 75–100 | 21–25 | 60–90 |
| 16–20 | 55–80 | 16–20 | 45–70 |
| 11–15 | 35–65 | 11–15 | 35–55 |
| 6–10 | 25–40 | 6–10 | 20–40 |
| 1–5 | 10–30 | 1–5 | 10–20 |
| 0 | 0 | 0 | 5 |

These score conversion tables are based on historical data from previously administered TOEIC tests. Therefore, your scores on the practice tests may be higher or lower than your scores on the actual TOEIC test.

NAME

## Listening Test

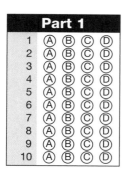

**Part 1**

| | |
|---|---|
| 1 | Ⓐ Ⓑ Ⓒ Ⓓ |
| 2 | Ⓐ Ⓑ Ⓒ Ⓓ |
| 3 | Ⓐ Ⓑ Ⓒ Ⓓ |
| 4 | Ⓐ Ⓑ Ⓒ Ⓓ |
| 5 | Ⓐ Ⓑ Ⓒ Ⓓ |
| 6 | Ⓐ Ⓑ Ⓒ Ⓓ |
| 7 | Ⓐ Ⓑ Ⓒ Ⓓ |
| 8 | Ⓐ Ⓑ Ⓒ Ⓓ |
| 9 | Ⓐ Ⓑ Ⓒ Ⓓ |
| 10 | Ⓐ Ⓑ Ⓒ Ⓓ |

**Part 2**

| | |
|---|---|
| 11 | Ⓐ Ⓑ Ⓒ |
| 12 | Ⓐ Ⓑ Ⓒ |
| 13 | Ⓐ Ⓑ Ⓒ |
| 14 | Ⓐ Ⓑ Ⓒ |
| 15 | Ⓐ Ⓑ Ⓒ |
| 16 | Ⓐ Ⓑ Ⓒ |
| 17 | Ⓐ Ⓑ Ⓒ |
| 18 | Ⓐ Ⓑ Ⓒ |
| 19 | Ⓐ Ⓑ Ⓒ |
| 20 | Ⓐ Ⓑ Ⓒ |
| 21 | Ⓐ Ⓑ Ⓒ |
| 22 | Ⓐ Ⓑ Ⓒ |
| 23 | Ⓐ Ⓑ Ⓒ |
| 24 | Ⓐ Ⓑ Ⓒ |
| 25 | Ⓐ Ⓑ Ⓒ |
| 26 | Ⓐ Ⓑ Ⓒ |
| 27 | Ⓐ Ⓑ Ⓒ |
| 28 | Ⓐ Ⓑ Ⓒ |
| 29 | Ⓐ Ⓑ Ⓒ |
| 30 | Ⓐ Ⓑ Ⓒ |
| 31 | Ⓐ Ⓑ Ⓒ |
| 32 | Ⓐ Ⓑ Ⓒ |
| 33 | Ⓐ Ⓑ Ⓒ |
| 34 | Ⓐ Ⓑ Ⓒ |
| 35 | Ⓐ Ⓑ Ⓒ |
| 36 | Ⓐ Ⓑ Ⓒ |
| 37 | Ⓐ Ⓑ Ⓒ |
| 38 | Ⓐ Ⓑ Ⓒ |
| 39 | Ⓐ Ⓑ Ⓒ |
| 40 | Ⓐ Ⓑ Ⓒ |

**Part 3**

| | |
|---|---|
| 41 | Ⓐ Ⓑ Ⓒ Ⓓ |
| 42 | Ⓐ Ⓑ Ⓒ Ⓓ |
| 43 | Ⓐ Ⓑ Ⓒ Ⓓ |
| 44 | Ⓐ Ⓑ Ⓒ Ⓓ |
| 45 | Ⓐ Ⓑ Ⓒ Ⓓ |
| 46 | Ⓐ Ⓑ Ⓒ Ⓓ |
| 47 | Ⓐ Ⓑ Ⓒ Ⓓ |
| 48 | Ⓐ Ⓑ Ⓒ Ⓓ |
| 49 | Ⓐ Ⓑ Ⓒ Ⓓ |
| 50 | Ⓐ Ⓑ Ⓒ Ⓓ |
| 51 | Ⓐ Ⓑ Ⓒ Ⓓ |
| 52 | Ⓐ Ⓑ Ⓒ Ⓓ |
| 53 | Ⓐ Ⓑ Ⓒ Ⓓ |
| 54 | Ⓐ Ⓑ Ⓒ Ⓓ |
| 55 | Ⓐ Ⓑ Ⓒ Ⓓ |
| 56 | Ⓐ Ⓑ Ⓒ Ⓓ |
| 57 | Ⓐ Ⓑ Ⓒ Ⓓ |
| 58 | Ⓐ Ⓑ Ⓒ Ⓓ |
| 59 | Ⓐ Ⓑ Ⓒ Ⓓ |
| 60 | Ⓐ Ⓑ Ⓒ Ⓓ |
| 61 | Ⓐ Ⓑ Ⓒ Ⓓ |
| 62 | Ⓐ Ⓑ Ⓒ Ⓓ |
| 63 | Ⓐ Ⓑ Ⓒ Ⓓ |
| 64 | Ⓐ Ⓑ Ⓒ Ⓓ |
| 65 | Ⓐ Ⓑ Ⓒ Ⓓ |
| 66 | Ⓐ Ⓑ Ⓒ Ⓓ |
| 67 | Ⓐ Ⓑ Ⓒ Ⓓ |
| 68 | Ⓐ Ⓑ Ⓒ Ⓓ |
| 69 | Ⓐ Ⓑ Ⓒ Ⓓ |
| 70 | Ⓐ Ⓑ Ⓒ Ⓓ |

**Part 4**

| | |
|---|---|
| 71 | Ⓐ Ⓑ Ⓒ Ⓓ |
| 72 | Ⓐ Ⓑ Ⓒ Ⓓ |
| 73 | Ⓐ Ⓑ Ⓒ Ⓓ |
| 74 | Ⓐ Ⓑ Ⓒ Ⓓ |
| 75 | Ⓐ Ⓑ Ⓒ Ⓓ |
| 76 | Ⓐ Ⓑ Ⓒ Ⓓ |
| 77 | Ⓐ Ⓑ Ⓒ Ⓓ |
| 78 | Ⓐ Ⓑ Ⓒ Ⓓ |
| 79 | Ⓐ Ⓑ Ⓒ Ⓓ |
| 80 | Ⓐ Ⓑ Ⓒ Ⓓ |
| 81 | Ⓐ Ⓑ Ⓒ Ⓓ |
| 82 | Ⓐ Ⓑ Ⓒ Ⓓ |
| 83 | Ⓐ Ⓑ Ⓒ Ⓓ |
| 84 | Ⓐ Ⓑ Ⓒ Ⓓ |
| 85 | Ⓐ Ⓑ Ⓒ Ⓓ |
| 86 | Ⓐ Ⓑ Ⓒ Ⓓ |
| 87 | Ⓐ Ⓑ Ⓒ Ⓓ |
| 88 | Ⓐ Ⓑ Ⓒ Ⓓ |
| 89 | Ⓐ Ⓑ Ⓒ Ⓓ |
| 90 | Ⓐ Ⓑ Ⓒ Ⓓ |
| 91 | Ⓐ Ⓑ Ⓒ Ⓓ |
| 92 | Ⓐ Ⓑ Ⓒ Ⓓ |
| 93 | Ⓐ Ⓑ Ⓒ Ⓓ |
| 94 | Ⓐ Ⓑ Ⓒ Ⓓ |
| 95 | Ⓐ Ⓑ Ⓒ Ⓓ |
| 96 | Ⓐ Ⓑ Ⓒ Ⓓ |
| 97 | Ⓐ Ⓑ Ⓒ Ⓓ |
| 98 | Ⓐ Ⓑ Ⓒ Ⓓ |
| 99 | Ⓐ Ⓑ Ⓒ Ⓓ |
| 100 | Ⓐ Ⓑ Ⓒ Ⓓ |

## Reading Test

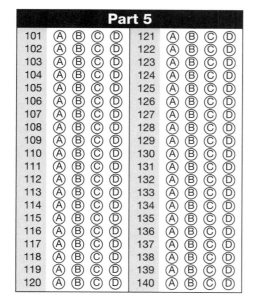

**Part 5**

| | | | |
|---|---|---|---|
| 101 | Ⓐ Ⓑ Ⓒ Ⓓ | 121 | Ⓐ Ⓑ Ⓒ Ⓓ |
| 102 | Ⓐ Ⓑ Ⓒ Ⓓ | 122 | Ⓐ Ⓑ Ⓒ Ⓓ |
| 103 | Ⓐ Ⓑ Ⓒ Ⓓ | 123 | Ⓐ Ⓑ Ⓒ Ⓓ |
| 104 | Ⓐ Ⓑ Ⓒ Ⓓ | 124 | Ⓐ Ⓑ Ⓒ Ⓓ |
| 105 | Ⓐ Ⓑ Ⓒ Ⓓ | 125 | Ⓐ Ⓑ Ⓒ Ⓓ |
| 106 | Ⓐ Ⓑ Ⓒ Ⓓ | 126 | Ⓐ Ⓑ Ⓒ Ⓓ |
| 107 | Ⓐ Ⓑ Ⓒ Ⓓ | 127 | Ⓐ Ⓑ Ⓒ Ⓓ |
| 108 | Ⓐ Ⓑ Ⓒ Ⓓ | 128 | Ⓐ Ⓑ Ⓒ Ⓓ |
| 109 | Ⓐ Ⓑ Ⓒ Ⓓ | 129 | Ⓐ Ⓑ Ⓒ Ⓓ |
| 110 | Ⓐ Ⓑ Ⓒ Ⓓ | 130 | Ⓐ Ⓑ Ⓒ Ⓓ |
| 111 | Ⓐ Ⓑ Ⓒ Ⓓ | 131 | Ⓐ Ⓑ Ⓒ Ⓓ |
| 112 | Ⓐ Ⓑ Ⓒ Ⓓ | 132 | Ⓐ Ⓑ Ⓒ Ⓓ |
| 113 | Ⓐ Ⓑ Ⓒ Ⓓ | 133 | Ⓐ Ⓑ Ⓒ Ⓓ |
| 114 | Ⓐ Ⓑ Ⓒ Ⓓ | 134 | Ⓐ Ⓑ Ⓒ Ⓓ |
| 115 | Ⓐ Ⓑ Ⓒ Ⓓ | 135 | Ⓐ Ⓑ Ⓒ Ⓓ |
| 116 | Ⓐ Ⓑ Ⓒ Ⓓ | 136 | Ⓐ Ⓑ Ⓒ Ⓓ |
| 117 | Ⓐ Ⓑ Ⓒ Ⓓ | 137 | Ⓐ Ⓑ Ⓒ Ⓓ |
| 118 | Ⓐ Ⓑ Ⓒ Ⓓ | 138 | Ⓐ Ⓑ Ⓒ Ⓓ |
| 119 | Ⓐ Ⓑ Ⓒ Ⓓ | 139 | Ⓐ Ⓑ Ⓒ Ⓓ |
| 120 | Ⓐ Ⓑ Ⓒ Ⓓ | 140 | Ⓐ Ⓑ Ⓒ Ⓓ |

**Part 6**

| | |
|---|---|
| 141 | Ⓐ Ⓑ Ⓒ Ⓓ |
| 142 | Ⓐ Ⓑ Ⓒ Ⓓ |
| 143 | Ⓐ Ⓑ Ⓒ Ⓓ |
| 144 | Ⓐ Ⓑ Ⓒ Ⓓ |
| 145 | Ⓐ Ⓑ Ⓒ Ⓓ |
| 146 | Ⓐ Ⓑ Ⓒ Ⓓ |
| 147 | Ⓐ Ⓑ Ⓒ Ⓓ |
| 148 | Ⓐ Ⓑ Ⓒ Ⓓ |
| 149 | Ⓐ Ⓑ Ⓒ Ⓓ |
| 150 | Ⓐ Ⓑ Ⓒ Ⓓ |
| 151 | Ⓐ Ⓑ Ⓒ Ⓓ |
| 152 | Ⓐ Ⓑ Ⓒ Ⓓ |

**Part 7**

| | | | |
|---|---|---|---|
| 153 | Ⓐ Ⓑ Ⓒ Ⓓ | 177 | Ⓐ Ⓑ Ⓒ Ⓓ |
| 154 | Ⓐ Ⓑ Ⓒ Ⓓ | 178 | Ⓐ Ⓑ Ⓒ Ⓓ |
| 155 | Ⓐ Ⓑ Ⓒ Ⓓ | 179 | Ⓐ Ⓑ Ⓒ Ⓓ |
| 156 | Ⓐ Ⓑ Ⓒ Ⓓ | 180 | Ⓐ Ⓑ Ⓒ Ⓓ |
| 157 | Ⓐ Ⓑ Ⓒ Ⓓ | 181 | Ⓐ Ⓑ Ⓒ Ⓓ |
| 158 | Ⓐ Ⓑ Ⓒ Ⓓ | 182 | Ⓐ Ⓑ Ⓒ Ⓓ |
| 159 | Ⓐ Ⓑ Ⓒ Ⓓ | 183 | Ⓐ Ⓑ Ⓒ Ⓓ |
| 160 | Ⓐ Ⓑ Ⓒ Ⓓ | 184 | Ⓐ Ⓑ Ⓒ Ⓓ |
| 161 | Ⓐ Ⓑ Ⓒ Ⓓ | 185 | Ⓐ Ⓑ Ⓒ Ⓓ |
| 162 | Ⓐ Ⓑ Ⓒ Ⓓ | 186 | Ⓐ Ⓑ Ⓒ Ⓓ |
| 163 | Ⓐ Ⓑ Ⓒ Ⓓ | 187 | Ⓐ Ⓑ Ⓒ Ⓓ |
| 164 | Ⓐ Ⓑ Ⓒ Ⓓ | 188 | Ⓐ Ⓑ Ⓒ Ⓓ |
| 165 | Ⓐ Ⓑ Ⓒ Ⓓ | 189 | Ⓐ Ⓑ Ⓒ Ⓓ |
| 166 | Ⓐ Ⓑ Ⓒ Ⓓ | 190 | Ⓐ Ⓑ Ⓒ Ⓓ |
| 167 | Ⓐ Ⓑ Ⓒ Ⓓ | 191 | Ⓐ Ⓑ Ⓒ Ⓓ |
| 168 | Ⓐ Ⓑ Ⓒ Ⓓ | 192 | Ⓐ Ⓑ Ⓒ Ⓓ |
| 169 | Ⓐ Ⓑ Ⓒ Ⓓ | 193 | Ⓐ Ⓑ Ⓒ Ⓓ |
| 170 | Ⓐ Ⓑ Ⓒ Ⓓ | 194 | Ⓐ Ⓑ Ⓒ Ⓓ |
| 171 | Ⓐ Ⓑ Ⓒ Ⓓ | 195 | Ⓐ Ⓑ Ⓒ Ⓓ |
| 172 | Ⓐ Ⓑ Ⓒ Ⓓ | 196 | Ⓐ Ⓑ Ⓒ Ⓓ |
| 173 | Ⓐ Ⓑ Ⓒ Ⓓ | 197 | Ⓐ Ⓑ Ⓒ Ⓓ |
| 174 | Ⓐ Ⓑ Ⓒ Ⓓ | 198 | Ⓐ Ⓑ Ⓒ Ⓓ |
| 175 | Ⓐ Ⓑ Ⓒ Ⓓ | 199 | Ⓐ Ⓑ Ⓒ Ⓓ |
| 176 | Ⓐ Ⓑ Ⓒ Ⓓ | 200 | Ⓐ Ⓑ Ⓒ Ⓓ |

Tactics for TOEIC® Listening and Reading Test  **Practice Test 1**

**OXFORD**

UNIVERSITY PRESS

www.oup.com/elt

OXFORD ENGLISH
ISBN 978-0-19-452955-6

9 780194 529556